DOG HEROES

Saving Lives and Protecting America

JEN BIDNER

The Lyons Press
Guilford, Connecticut
An imprint of The Globe Pequot Press

CONTENTS

ACKNOWLEDGMENTS

I would like to thank the many people who made this book possible

Editorial and Conceptual Help

I offer many thanks to Meleda Lowry for her photographic help, and for accompanying me on my cross-country road trip to take the pictures; Dr. Fred J. Heinritz and Anne Bidner for their insightful critiques and copy suggestions; Jo Bidner for help photo editing; and the talented staff of The Lyons Press who helped bring this book to fruition.

Dog Handlers, Trainers, and Instructors

I would like to express my appreciation to the trainers and dog handlers who shared their expertise and allowed me to photograph their dogs. Among them were (in alphabetical order): Kathy Albrecht (PetHunters), Jerry Balint (Jackson Ski Patrol), Wendy Beltz (USDA), Pam Bennet (TRASAR), Lt. Chris Carpenter (AR Game & Fish), Cil Chenevert (Leominster EMA, MA), Sgt. Mark Combes (Perry PD, OK) and Dr. Gayla Combes DVM, Bill Dotson, Joseph Falman (TASK-9), Amir Findling (WNYSAR), Charm Gentry (WV K-9 FACT), Patti Gibson (ILL-WIS SAR), Kim Gilmore (Flathead County SAR), Behesha Grist (Shuler Mantrailing Seminars), Shirley Hammond (CA-TF-3), Tricia Heldmann (TASK-9), Nancy Hook (REDS), Det. Jonni Joyce (RDU Airport Police), Marcia Koenig (King County Search Dogs), Marci Larson, Mary MacQueen (Nitro Golden Retrievers), Lisa Mayhew (Office of the Chief Medical Examiner, NC), Nan Lux (Search Dogs NE), Geri Messina (ILL-WIS SAR), Karen Nesbitt (Leominster EMA, MA), Lucy Newton, Newfound Friends Foundation, Karen Ogden, Alison Pae (USDA), Ret. Off. William Proulx (East Hartford PD, CT), Ken Pullen, Vicki Pulver (ILL-WIS SAR), Andy Rebmann (Cadaver Dog Handbook), Heather Roche, Bryan Ryndak (ILL-WIS SAR), Calvin Shuler, Jr. (USDA), Jack Shuler (Shuler Mantrailing Seminars), Robin Siggers (Fernie Ski Patrol), Beckie Stanevich (TRASAR), Pat Thompson, Cpl. Frankie Tucker (AR Game & Fish), Dan Vice (USDA), Chief Waters (RDU Airport Police), Bob Watson (REDS), Dep. Kimberly Watson (Jack Co. Sheriffs Dept., TX), Mitzi Webber (FL TF-1), Ann Wichmann (CO-TF-1), Janet Wilts (National Park Service), and others.

Other Expertise and Help

I would like to thank Tricia Heldmann and the members of TASK-9 for their training and companionship; Jonni Joyce for endless instruction and training advice; Sue Bentley for acting as training assistant for my trailing dog; the divers of Innerspace Explorers and Gillman Dive Clubs for their volunteer water training work; and Dr. Fred J. Heinritz for his constant aid assisting with dogs.

All WWI and earlier historical data is from Col. E.H. Richard's several books on dogs. The WWII information is from U.S. government statistics.

INTRODUCTION

There are thousands of search dogs and handlers in the United States working to protect and save lives

Government and Police Dogs

Many of the nation's best detection dog and handler teams are paid professionals, employed by state, federal, and local government agencies, law enforcement and fire departments, and all branches of the Armed Forces.

Volunteer Dog Teams

Hundreds of volunteer members of search units are dispersed across the country—even in Alaska and Hawaii. Some are able to get corporate and private sponsors, but most volunteer handlers foot the bill for their own expenses, which can be quite high.

Myriad Specialties

Some readers may be surprised to learn the wide role dogs play, from traditional specialties such as narcotics detection and man-tracking, to the novel areas of termite and cancer detection.

As public awareness grows about the incredible olfactory capabilities of dogs, I am confident that even more new and unusual specialties will be developed by researchers in cooperation with dog handlers.

It is important to note that while some dogs are cross-trained to several specialties, no dog can "do it all." Many handlers choose to become specialists, concentrating all their training efforts in one or two directions. In the same way you would not hire a brain surgeon to do your heart bypass, a search commander must utilize dog teams according to how their individual specialities are appropriate for solving the task at hand.

Getting Started in Search and Rescue

Be forewarned: Search and rescue is a very rewarding activity, but it can also be extremely demanding from a mental, physical and financial standpoint.

Though this book offers insights on how dogs and handlers are trained, it is not designed to be a how-to text. If you think you might want to get involved in volunteer canine search and rescue, check out the list of ten considerations and the recommended reading list in the "Getting Started" chapter beginning on page 113.

Man has relied on the scenting capabilities of dogs for centuries

History and literature record the deeds of war dogs as early as 2,500 years ago, both as fighting troops and as sentries who scented the distant approach of enemies

Trailing bloodhounds (page 18) are descended from the Middle Ages, when many villages had hounds trained to hunt down criminals.

Air-scenting dogs (page 26) take their tradition from the famed dogs of the St. Bernard and other alpine passes, where they patrolled independently, looking for the lost and injured, and reporting their finds to their handlers.

Modern cadaver dog training is based on the "ambu-lance dog" of the turn of the century. These dogs were taught to differentiate between the dead and the wounded, but to alert only on the living, while the cadaver dog is trained to alert only on the dead.

Newfoundlands were originally bred as lifesaving dogs (page 67), who would search the seacoast for drowning sailors, and drag them to shore.

Customs Agency dogs (page 94) have a history going back over one hundred years, when the French used dogs to stop the smuggling of tobacco and lace over the border. Some clever smugglers used dogs to carry the goods, while customs dogs were expected to stop and kill them.

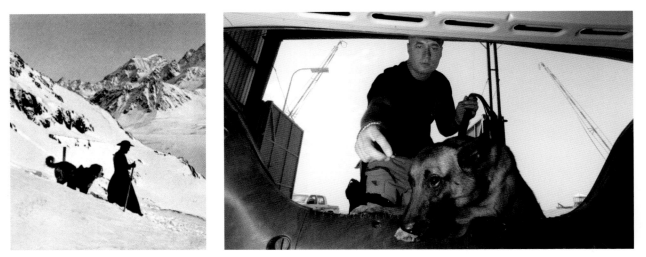

During WWI, when artillery could easily knock out communications equipment, messenger dogs were perhaps the most valued of all war dogs

Systematized war dog training

By the time of the Franco-Prussian War (1870-1871), Germany already had an advanced system of military and police dog training.

Russian war dogs were well established by the time of the Russo-Japanese War in 1905. Their guard dogs were instrumental in protecting the entire length of the Trans-Siberian Railroad by alerting soldiers of ambushes well in advance. Holland, Sweden, and Italy followed shortly thereafter, developing organized dog training systems.

Ambulance dogs rescued the wounded

By 1900, European armies were using dogs to help stretcher-bearers find the wounded on the battlefield. These dogs would usually work off-lead and remain with the wounded man and bark an alert, or bring back a hat or other token of their find, or simply return to the handler and run back and forth between the two.

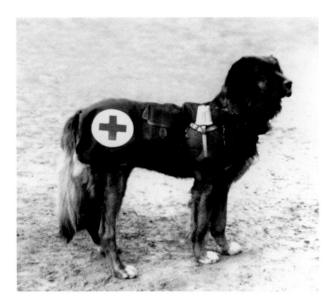

Gear for WWI ambulance dogs

German ambulance dogs (*sanitshunds*) wore saddles with pockets that held bandages and dressings, and had barrels around their necks with "stimulants." Italian dogs (left) also had saddles that were dominated by large flask pockets. The Russians provided their dogs with lanterns (right).

Col. E.H. Richardson, England's most famous dog trainer of WWI, preferred to dress British dogs lightly with just a red cross vest and a collar with a bell (below).

With the threat of chemical weapons, valuable war dogs were also equipped with gas masks (below right).

Two dogs trained by Col. Richardson, loaned to Russia in 1905 for use in the Russo-Japanese War

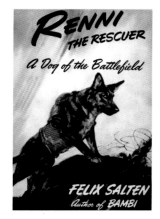

Rescue dogs were crowd-pleasers

Ambulance dogs caught the fancy of the public. Countless newspapers and magazines reported their heroic deeds, and they were the fictional heroes of many novels from WWI through the 1950s.

The invaluable messenger dog

Though not specifically a "search" dog, messenger dogs had to use their scenting instincts to navigate the ever-changing battlefield, find their message recipients and return home again

These dogs could travel the ground three to four times faster than a human runner, and do it in complete darkness. The casualty rate was extremely high for these dogs, and they were often sent out in packs with the hope that at least some would escape enemy fire.

War dogs had to be bold and fearless

Above, British WWI dogs are being trained to ignore rifle fire. At the start of the war, Britain had few military dogs. But by the end of the war, they were producing fully trained ambulance, messenger, sentry, and guard dogs. They continued their training efforts between the wars, and loaned the United States government many dogs at the start of WWII, before this country began its own training programs.

Man has been the legitimate "quarry" of bloodhounds for hundreds of years

Col. Richardson (right) pointed this out and argued that these dogs were unmatched because they had been selectively bred as mantrackers for over five hundred years. According to his research, they were so revered that the Royal Kennel of France was annually stocked with hounds from the Abbey of St. Hubert in Ardennes as early as 1202.

Disaster dogs got their start during the devastating air raids of WWII

In London, the Civil Defense units used rescue dogs to quickly search the rubble of collapsed buildings after air raids. All over Europe, military dogs (above) served the same function.

American dogs

During the Civil War, both the North and the South used messenger, guard, and tracking dogs. However, most of these dogs were brought to the war by individual soldiers in the same way many rode the family horse into battle. Stray dogs were quickly recruited into the ranks.

Bloodhounds were also reportedly used to track Seminole Indians in the Seminole Wars (circa 1841) and by the Rough Riders in the Spanish-American War (1898).

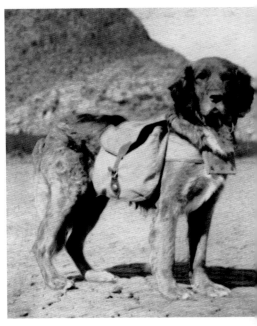

By the turn of the century, Americans were well-known for their tracking dogs. Unlike the English bloodhound that worked on-lead, American dogs were often let loose in packs, with the handlers following on horseback. This allowed them to quickly cover even the roughest country.

By the early 1900s, these dog packs were a common sight at prisons or guarding work camps. The system had its historic roots in the Southern plantations, where dogs were used to track down runaway slaves.

Despite a strong history of police and prison dogs at the turn of the century, the U.S. did not have an official war dog program until 1944 Once the decision was made to train U.S. war dogs, it came on a large scale. The Army Quartermaster Corps trained over ten thousand war dogs during WWII. Over three thousand of these dogs went to the Coast Guard to help guard our coastlines.

The importance of the scout dog increased during the Vietnam War, where the jungle terrain made ambushes hard to avoid without the advanced warning given by dogs.

Dogs have been used to hunt criminals through the ages

Landowners, townsmen, sheriffs, and prison guards have historically used dogs to track criminals, but the concept of a "police dog" is fairly new.

St. Malo, France, was a rare exception, and already had an organized police dog program as early as 1770. By the late 1800s, Belgium and Germany had police dogs nationwide. And by 1900, prisons in the U.S. regularly utilized dogs to chase down escapees, often running the dogs off-lead in packs.

In England, Col. Richardson developed two separate types of police dogs. The "executive" dog was tasked with night patrol, working to warn, guard, capture, and attack. The "criminal tracking" dogs were specialists brought in to follow the trails of criminals. As early as 1910, the results of these dogs' efforts were being used in trials as evidence to link criminals to crime scenes.

U.S. police and sheriff dogs were world-renowned for their ability to track fleeing horsemen for miles.

NY State Police had the first specialized cadaver dog in 1974

According to cadaver dog specialist Andrew Rebmann, Trooper Jim Suffolk (New York State Police) handled a yellow lab named Pearl, who became the first police dog to specialize in human remains detection as a law enforcement tool. In 1977, Rebmann helped initiate a cadaver dog program with the Connecticut State Police.

Police dogs have long been a part of state police departments. Below is a photo believed to be of the New York State Police, probably in the Utica area, circa 1915. Note the German shepherd patrol dog, and the pit bull puppy.

TRACKING & TRAILING

Following a person's path of travel with dogs is the oldest search specialty, with a history going back centuries

Dogs can be used to follow a person hours, days, or sometimes more than a week later—even after rain or snow has wiped out every visible trace

It might sound like fiction, but well-trained trailing dogs can sometimes follow the scent of a person who travelled in the area ten or more days earlier. Because they are following the scent of a specific person, they can ignore "scent contamination" from hundreds of people, animals or cars that have crossed the path during that time.

Tracking vs. Trailing—What's the Difference?

Tracking dogs follow footprints, whereas trailing dogs follow the scent wherever it has drifted, regardless of where the feet are placed (or not). In the 1930s a tramlike device (left) was created to demonstrate that trailing dogs could follow a person who never touched the ground

Professional K-9 Instructor Jonni Joyce describes these two different specialties:

"*Tracking* dogs follow footsteps, smelling the disturbance in vegetation and sedimentation created by the landing of the foot on the ground. The tracking dog is supposed to keep its nose to the ground and stay close to the actual path followed. The dog is not given a scent article. If another person crosses the track, the dog is expected to discriminate the difference in ground odor rather than the difference in human scent.

Tracking dogs are incapable of working in an area contaminated by other people. Once the ground disturbances disappear, they are no longer able to follow the track. Tracking is often used by law enforcement in 'hot pursuits' where the dog is following the person who just ran away. Tracking is also a show-ring sport.

"*Trailing* dogs, on the other hand, are trained on human odor and are not required to keep their nose to the ground. They may work at a distance from the actual path of travel (the footsteps), because the scent of the person is affected by wind, weather and terrain conditions, and may have drifted.

"Trailers are given an object that was last touched by the subject (a scent article) and are expected to differentiate that scent from all others. Therefore they can work in areas contaminated by many people."

Trailing in an urban environment is more difficult than in pristine wilderness

Several factors make urban trailing one of the most difficult search specialities. The area is generally contaminated with the scent of other people, dogs, cars, and trash. This requires the dog to concentrate harder to separate out the "right" scent. Secondly, while vegetation tends to catch and hold the scent in place, the scent seems to "skate" along asphalt and concrete. One will often see urban trailing dogs following the edge of curbs or buildings, or checking cracks in the sidewalk—all places that "catch" the scent and allow it to settle. The third factor is heat. Asphalt quickly heats up in the summer, burning dogs' paws and destroying the residual scent.

Search dog training needs to be done in realistic settings, so many trailing teams train on city streets. The person "laying" the trail takes a walk and then hides. Dep. Kimberly Watson (Jack Co. Sheriffs Dept., TX) tells the story of one such training: The trail-layer traveled down several streets before hiding under a table in her post office's off-hours area.

During the wait, a citizen entered to get her mail. Seeing the prone person, the woman walked over to get a closer look. Trying to explain why she was hiding in the dark, the trail-layer said, "They're tracking me with bloodhounds." The citizen bolted from the post office and, spotting the approaching dog team, frantically pointed to where she'd left the "criminal," calling *"Hurry! She's in there!"*

Trailing dogs are taught to scent-discriminate

They are presented with a scent article or source and asked to follow only that scent. One of the most difficult aspects of this work is obtaining a good scent article!

The dog is usually trained to follow the freshest scent on the scent article (other than the handler's). So if someone gives it to the handler, the freshest scent belongs to the giver. The dog would then have to be brought to the giver so he could be ruled out as providing the "original" scent.

Despite popular belief, you don't need an odoriferous item like a smelly sock for the dog to catch the scent. A piece of sterile gauze laid on a car seat for a few seconds is enough! Fabric and porous items hold scent better than slick surfaces like metal, but one can still scent a dog on a key or a car door. Dogs can even pick up a scent off one drop of dried blood.

Practiced dogs can tell the difference between family members—even twins, despite the family resemblance of the scents.

Dogs really can smell "fear"

As one police officer describes it: "Fear scent lights up the trail for the dog like a neon light!"

Any criminal fleeing from the police is bound to start giving off "fear scent," a sour sweat probably caused by adrenaline in the body. It is such a part of criminal search that an artificial "fear scent" is manufactured for the purpose of training dogs. (It is difficult to naturally produce fear scent in training because the subject knows he is not in any real danger.)

It is important to note that not all tracking or trailing subjects will be fearful. Children under the age of three and Alzheimer's patients are often unaware that they are lost or in jeopardy.

Most tracking and trailing dogs work in a harness on-lead, but some work off-lead

While most tracking and trailing dogs work in a harness with a lead from ten to thirty feet long, some wilderness trailing dogs are taught to track off-lead. It is considered a time-saver for handlers, because the dogs can run ahead. When they find the subject, they then "refind" the handler and tell them what they have found (through a trained action like a bark or tag), and then take the handler back to the victim at a more human pace.

This is a dangerous activity in urban settings because even streetwise dogs may charge blindly across a street when "on-scent" and distracted. Sadly, many police handlers who have released their dogs to pursue a criminal have learned this the painful way, when their dogs were killed by police or civilian cars.

Most tracking and trailing dogs perform a trained action to positively identify the subject when they find him

In law enforcement it is important that the dog is trained to positively identify the object of the search (the subject ID). Often this involves the dog "tagging" the suspect with a paw indicating to the handler that this is the person the dog was told to look for (especially if the finish is in a crowded area). This is an action that the officer can describe in a courtroom, to prove that his dog isn't just walking up to everyone in his path.

In civilian search, subject ID is not as imperative since one usually has a description of the lost person, and it is obvious when he's been found. However, runaway teens, publicity seekers, and confused Alzheimer's patients have been known to "sneak" back into the base camp to watch all the action. Without a trained "finish" to the problem, the handler might scold the dog and tell him to get back to work when he follows the trail right up to this person. The trained finish also helps provide a clear close to the exercise and a point at which to reward the dog.

Common subject IDs include tagging the subject with the paw or a "refind" in which the dog turns around and tags the handler. Bloodhounds are notorious for putting their paws on a standing search subject's shoulders—an intimidating action popular with police handlers!

Mika (left) demonstrates an airborne version of this on her handler, Geri Messina of the ILL-WIS SAR Dog unit.

This young lab shows his enthusiasm for his work as he joyfully finds his subject

Bloodhounds have been used as man-trailers for hundreds of years

At the turn of the century, American railroad detectives (left) used bloodhounds to track criminals.

However, their lineage alone does not guarantee success. One still needs to pick a bloodhound that shows the right traits and the desire to work, and then train him well to be assured of success.

They might not look like athletes under all those folds of skin, but well-conditioned bloodhounds are relentless in their pursuit.

The ten-mile trail

In Effington County, Illinois, a recently released convict waited in his mother's car in the parking lot of the bar where she worked. When she came out he asked her for money. Unfortunately, their discussion abruptly ended when he shot her in the head and then fled the scene.

Forty hours later, Jack Shuler, a deputy with the Marion Co. Sheriffs Dept., was called to the scene. Law enforcement already had a suspect identified, but they wanted to see if Jack's bloodhound could link the crime scene to him via the dog's nose.

Jack placed sterile gauze on the passenger seat of the car to pick up the scent of the last person who sat there. He then scented the dog off the gauze, and set off on the trail. The dog followed a railroad track for a distance, over track ties that had been replaced during the forty hours since the suspect left the trail.

The police stopped Jack as he and the bloodhound closed in on a house. Unbeknownst to Jack, it turned out that this was where the son lived, and the Sheriffs Department was staking it out.

An eleven-day-old trail helps find a missing homicide victim

Foul play was suspected when a young mother disappeared and the primary suspect fled the country. Bloodhound Dixie was assigned to try and find a trail from the place he was last seen

All the cards seemed to be stacked against Vicki Pulver (from ILL-WIS SAR Dogs unit) and her bloodhound Dixie: The trail was eleven days old and the area had seen almost three inches of heavy rain during that time.

To compound problems, the suspect's apartment had probably been contaminated by other people during the week, making the collection of a "pure" scent article diffi-

cult. Vicki needed to be sure she scented the dog off the suspect and not a bystander. Therefore she placed a sterile gauze pad between the mattress and the box spring to absorb the person's scent.

A witness had seen the suspect cross a pasture fence near the apartment on the day the woman went missing. Vicki scented her dog in the area. After circling a few times, Dixie gave a strong pull in the harness and took off on the trail. Over the next three-quarters of a mile, the dog made several turns before ending up near a river.

Although following the scent of the suspect, Dixie, who is cross-trained in human remains detection, started giving strong indicators that she smelled a dead body. Vicki immediately called for two ILL-WIS SAR cadaver dog teams to start working the river. She took Dixie out of harness (to let her know she was no longer tracking the suspect) and gave her the cadaver command. Now off-lead, the bloodhound took off at a run and began following the scent clues coming off the body.

"The best part of this was the team work because two dogs were homing in on the victim at the same time," said Vicki afterwards.

"Dixie came over the last hill and we saw the woman's wrapped body near the edge of the river—and at almost the same time, Carol Lussky and Buddy arrived after working the river bank toward the scent."

Later, she found out that Vixen, who was working the opposite river bank with handler Janet Anagnos, was showing indications that she had detected the scent of body from across the river.

Many herding breeds like shepherds and Malinois often work with their head held high, rather than their nose on the ground

Wilderness dogs can quickly search a large area, looking for the scent coming off the actual missing person

Air-scent dogs usually wear vests, bells, and lights so that victims will not be frightened when a "huge wolf" barrels in at them

The search area is divided into large blocks, and dog teams are often deployed to search the most probable locations

Both the terrain and a dog's training determine how large an area the dog can effectively cover in a certain amount of time. In the Northeast, a typical initial search area is 40 acres for a dog with basic air-scenting skills and 160 acres for an advanced dog, and it is expected to be done in under two hours (and usually much less). In the open plains, a much larger area can be covered in that time, but in the mountains or dense forest it might be far less.

Most air-scent teams search for any human scent, which means their search area should be cleared of personnel and bystanders before beginning (because the dog doesn't know the difference between rescuers and the victim). If a scent article is available for the missing person, an air-scenting dog trained to scent-discriminate can be used without clearing the area.

In training, dogs must practice with a wide range of subjects. If he's used to finding one "training victim" sitting on a rock every time, in a real search the dog may not alert to groups or a running, unconscious, or otherwise "unexpected" victim type.

If there is no trail to follow, air-scenting dogs can be used to quickly "clear" large sectors of woodland

The handler then usually works the area in a systematic grid, sometimes walking the perimeter first. As the handler walks the grid, the dog does the "leg work," ranging away from the handler at a run, checking all the land on either side. The dog's distance from the handler varies according to the terrain and the individual style of the team.

Air-scenting dogs must be confident, agile and bold

Much of a dog's training is spent teaching him what to do after he finds the victim

The dog may be a great distance away from the handler at that time and must somehow communicate what he has found

If the victim is in the assigned search area, and the handler is gridding properly for the wind and terrain, the well-trained dog will eventually cross the scent of the person from the downwind side. On a windy day, the dog might catch this scent from a quarter mile or further away. The dog is then expected to follow the scent to its source.

Once the dog finds the victim, he must then communicate what he has found. Usually this is done by having the dog "refind" the handler, give a special signal (a trained alert), and then turn and take the handler back to the victim.

The "bark alert" is a common way of communicating this, and is easily recognized as Lassie's "Come quick! Timmy fell in the well!" bark. Other alerts include a "body bang" (in which the dog jumps up and bangs the handler), the "bringsel" (the dog takes a stick that is attached to his collar into his mouth), or the dog grabs a specific toy or towel off the handler's belt.

Other dogs are trained to pick up a nearby stick or object and bring it back to the handler to indicate that they have found the victim. This latter technique was popular with the "ambulance" or "mercy dogs" of World War I, who were trained to bring back the wounded soldier's hat or an article of clothing.

Another method is the bark-and-hold, in which the dog stays with the victim and barks—a technique often used with disaster specialty dogs. The drawback is that the barking might scare the victim, or that the barks might go unheard under wooded, windy or rainy conditions.

Air-scenting dogs work off-lead, often at great distances away from their handlers

Not Just Wilderness

Air-scenting dogs are often used for building searches

Many readers envision wilderness searches when they picture search dogs—but dogs can be used effectively inside a building. In the case of lost children, many times the parent is certain that the child has gotten lost outside, and "every inch of the house" has been checked. An air-scent dog can quickly verify this, and more than a few kids have been found hiding under the bed or in the attic. They were either there the entire time, or snuck back in and hid to avoid getting in trouble for all the commotion they caused.

Andy Rebmann (King Co. Search Dogs, WA) has found this to be especially true at nursing homes with Alzheimer's patients. They have found patients in locked rooms (the nursing staff assumed that because the door was locked the patient couldn't be inside), and broom closets. One patient, who had mistakenly crawled into another person's bed, was found, and another woman was rescued after three days spent in the furnace room.

When the dog hits the "scent cone" he will abruptly change direction and begin working a "Z" pattern toward the subject

In perfect search conditions, when wind hits the subject and blows his scent, it disperses in an ever widening cone (the "scent cone"). When the dog crosses this "scent cone" in the air, he instinctively turns and moves into it ("air-scenting"). When the scent stops at the opposite edge of the cone, the dog turns back into it. This creates a zig-zag pattern that becomes narrower and narrower as the dog zeroes in toward the tip of the cone and the source of the scent.

In the real world, terrain, weather conditions, and changing wind directions can break up the scent or send it in a course that is far from a perfect cone shape. This can make it exponentially more difficult for the dog to follow. Chimneying, for example, occurs when a localized air current carries the scent straight up in the air, only to have it land in spots several feet or huge distances away. The dog (and handler) must learn to understand these phenomena.

Snow, rain, hail, extreme heat and nightfall affect success

Small amounts of snow can actually make the search easier because tracks are more visible, and scenting conditions are often good. But while the handlers can slip on snowshoes or skis, deep snow hinders dogs' ability to move and quickly exhausts them. The cold can also be life-threatening to the unprepared lost person.

Likewise, light rain can keep both handler and dog cool, but conversely it can quickly cause hypothermia in a victim without rain gear—even in warm weather.

Many searches must be run at night to avoid losing precious time finding a victim. Surprisingly, dog handlers often find that the scenting conditions at night are actually better. For the dog, who works with his nose and not his eyes, the darkness is not a hindrance.

It is important to note that search dogs tend to be very stoic, and will work even when injured, overheated or dehydrated. Handlers must therefore be extremely careful to monitor their dog's health status in the field.

Rise in Alzheimer's searches

Alzheimer's patients often travel where others would not. They are notorious for walking straight into blackberry bushes or thickets until they get stuck. "For some reason, many never realize they can back up," said Andy Rebmann (King County Search Dogs). "I had a case where the man kept walking in place, not realizing he was stuck, so that he actually wore a pit in the ground."

King County Search Dogs is just one search unit that has noticed an increase in searches related to Alzheimer's disease. Almost one third of their sixty-six searches in 2001 were for Alzheimer's patients.

A memorable example was a search by Lafond Davis and Sunny. They were searching along a chain-link fence when the dog became agitated. He did not give his trained refind behavior, but offered enough body language for Davis to know he had found something. Sure enough, the subject was on the other side of the fence, snagged deep in some blackberry bushes!

Wanting to figure out why this experienced dog didn't do his full alert, the team later recreated the scenario in training. It turns out that the dog was confused because he could not reach the person due to the physical barrier. This was an important learning experience, and the unit added physical barriers to its regular training. Luckily, Davis was experienced enough to read her dog's body language and find the subject.

Search dogs must look *everywhere!*

Kidding aside, most seasoned handlers can tell you stories of unexpected places they have found their victims. Kids sometimes end up in car trunks, and Alzheimer's patients are notorious for traveling further than imaginable. For example, Alzheimer's patients might end up miles from home, while trying to follow the hunting trails of their youth.

DISASTER DOGS

Hundreds of dog teams responded to the World Trade Center collapse

The Federal Emergency Management Agency (FEMA) brought in specially trained disaster dog teams from around the country

We heard the shocking news of the terrorist attacks on the morning of September 11, 2001. But unlike the rest of us who sat down, dizzied and stunned by the news, the men and women on FEMA urban task forces began rushing around their houses, checking their "ready packs" and stacking their gear by the door. These canine handlers had trained for years for an event they hoped would never come.

FEMA dogs work "naked"

They don't wear collars or vests that can get caught on twisted metal, or boots that would reduce their traction and eliminate the use of their claws.

Working off-leash, the dogs respond to their handlers' voices and hand commands. They are taught to navigate the rubble slowly, taking small steps rather than the more instinctive leaps that could displace debris and result in deadly falls.

FEMA's Urban Search and Rescue Task Forces

Dog teams are just one specialization in the Federal Emergency Management Agency's USAR task force system. There are twenty-seven of these task forces spread around the country. Each has sixty-two specialists, including four dog handlers. Each task force is self-sufficient with all necessary equipment and supplies, and can arrive on scene within hours.

A FEMA dog calmly rides a
makeshift tram across the
World Trade Center rubble

FEMA dogs are trained to alert only on the living so that precious rescue resources in the first seventy-two hours are focused on those who might be saved

Sunny (left) is the son of Spice, who worked at the Oklahoma City bombing in 1995

"Sunny is trained to do at least thirty seconds of sustained barking when he finds a live victim; and trained not to do that for the dead," Shirley Hammond, a twenty-year veteran of K9 disaster work, explains about FEMA canine standards. Even so, many of these dogs used body language to communicate when they'd found a body.

In one instance at Ground Zero, when Sunny started pawing the ground, the nearby Battalion Chief asked what that meant.

"He only barks on live finds," Shirley said, "but he wants me to know that something is there."

"That'll do," replied the chief, and the rescuers moved in.

At lunchtime one of the firemen found her and put his hand on her shoulder. "He told me that they'd found one of their own in a rubble grave below where Sunny was digging—and he wanted to thank us. I'm just glad I had enough experience to trust my dog," added Shirley.

Two decades of disaster dogs

Twenty years ago, long before the days of FEMA urban task forces, Shirley Hammond had already begun training dogs for disaster rescue. She and her first disaster dog Cinnamon worked in Mexico City after the devastating earthquakes in 1985, along with her husband David, who was a safety officer. They were both an integral part of the development of FEMA's training standards in the early 1990s, helping to modernize the nation's disaster readiness for the new era of the high-rise building. Today, the U.S. has one of the world's most advanced disaster rescue systems.

It is interesting to note that not all the urban task forces were deployed to New York City or the Pentagon, for strategic reasons—some must always be left in reserve to respond to other threats or natural disasters related or unrelated to the terrorist strikes.

At the age of sixty-eight, Shirley has decided she will soon leave the rubble climbing to the "younger kids," and retire as a FEMA handler. She's not quitting the search business, however. Instead, she'll focus on cadaver dogs and continue teaching other handlers.

Across New York Harbor from the World Trade Center, over fifty dog teams checked countless truckloads of debris for human remains before it was buried in landfill on Staten Island

The New York Office of Emergency Planning (OEP) called dozens of cadaver dog teams into action at the Fresh Kills landfill in Staten Island, New York City. Rubble was sent there in an endless line of trucks and barges from Ground Zero, and the dogs were being asked to find body parts that rescue workers were unable to locate or identify. The goal of this important work was to help forensic anthropologists identify additional victims and return their remains to the families.

"Without the dogs, we wouldn't have been able to distinguish human remains from other debris, because everything was covered in pulverized dust," reported one of the handlers. "It was grim work, but we were glad to be able to give some of the families closure."

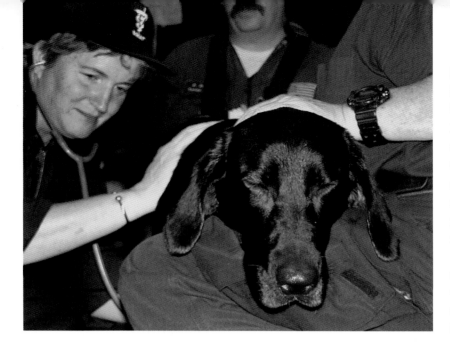

No search dogs died during the rescue efforts at the World Trade Center disaster Rubble is a very dangerous environment for even highly trained dogs. Frequent vet checks (left), postwork decontamination (at the Pentagon, near right), and plenty of water breaks (bottom right) are mandatory when working.

When pushed to extremes, disaster dogs can succumb to dehydration. Medics (far right) administer an IV to an ailing dog in the field.

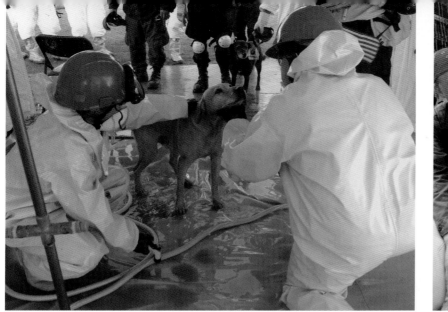

It takes about two years to train an advanced disaster dog

Good disaster dogs come in all shapes and sizes. Success depends upon their training and individual drives, not their breed.

Both big and small dogs have their advantages. A large dog can quickly traverse the rubble on his own, but his greater weight makes it more likely that debris will shift perilously. Small dogs can access smaller pockets and tunnels, can easily be lifted onto other surfaces, and are less likely to disturb rubble above a buried victim. On the other hand, they cannot navigate the bigger debris as well as larger dogs. The real trick is knowing one's dog, his capabilities and his limitations. The handler who has a good understanding of this is an asset to any search unit.

An escalator becomes as hazardous as a cliff

Exhausted search dogs "catnapped" whenever and wherever they could—a luxury that eluded many of their handlers

Usually, the Urban Search and Rescue (USAR) task force shifts run twelve hours on, twelve hours off. Physical exhaustion quickly sets in from the exertion of working in heavy gear in a dangerous environment, compounded by the mental stress of dealing with the enormity of the crisis and the emotions that come with it.

Dog handlers have the added burden of keeping their spirits and hopes up, because dogs are intuitive about their handler's emotions. Positive thinking keeps the dogs "in the game."

"Yes, the dogs work to please you. But the best dogs work because they love the hunt, and you need to let them know they're hunting well—even if they're not finding any survivors," explains one handler. "You need to keep them jazzed, even in the eleventh hour of a shift." Most handlers will agree that, regardless of how somber the actual search is to humans, the best dogs view search and rescue as their absolute favorite "game".

Bomb dog Sirius died in Tower 2 collapse

His handler, Officer David Lim, was trapped for five hours in collapsed Tower 1 with members of Ladder Company 6 and a woman they were aiding. They were able to scramble to Level 6 (the new ceiling), and climb down on ropes tossed up by other rescuers.

Sirius was a highly trained bomb-detection dog, who spent his days guarding the World Trade Center by checking incoming supply trucks for explosives. He and his handler, Port Authority Police Officer David Lim, were in Tower 2 when the first plane hit the other tower. Officer Lim, put the dog in his basement kennel for "safekeeping" while he went to help. That was the last time he saw the yellow lab, his partner and friend.

Sirius and thirty-seven Port Authority officers lost their lives on September 11. Officer Lim is now back to work with Sprig, his new bomb-detection dog.

An FDNY dog takes a break during recovery efforts

Although FEMA dogs were the disaster specialists, police and fire K9 played a vital role as well. Some police and fire K9 are regularly trained as first responders to disasters, practicing on rubble piles and doing human remains detection work. Many, however, had little or no experience prior to the call, and had to get on-the-job training to learn what their handlers needed. All worked hard in an extremely difficult situation.

FEMA, police, and fire dogs also served the dual role of morale boosters

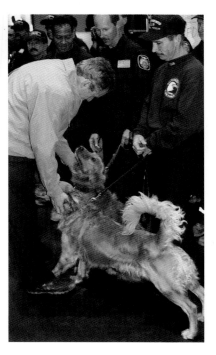

Sunny, Shirley Hammond's fierce-looking ninety-five-pound Doberman pinscher (page 40) was a magnet for rescue workers coming off shift or taking breaks.

"Although he's friendly, most people are normally afraid of him. Not here. These guys just wanted to—needed to—put their hands on him," said Shirley. "Some just came over to talk to the dog rather than me. They'd pet him for a while, whisper something to him, and then go back to work."

The Pentagon presented different problems for the rescuers than Ground Zero

Though smaller in scale than the World Trade Center, the rescue and recovery efforts at the Pentagon (right and below) were not easy. As seen below, even a partial building collapse is perilous for both dog and human rescue personnel.

FEMA dogs, such as the one at right, were used to look for survivors, while cadaver dogs followed to identify human remains.

In addition, dog teams were used in Pennsylvania to locate the remains of the passengers and crew of United Airlines Flight 93.

Three out of five of Ann's black labs are FEMA-certified disaster dogs

When the call came, Ann Wichmann and
two of her FEMA-certified dogs, Jenner and Merlyn,
joined Colorado Task Force One at the
World Trade Center site

Eight months after the collapse of the World Trade Center, Ann still has a hacking cough even though she used the highest quality respirators for her work.

"We had to remove our masks if we wanted to give our dogs verbal commands that they could actually hear," she explains. Her dogs seem none the worse for wear, however.

Below, she sets out for a hard day of searching at Ground Zero with Jenner, her oldest black Labrador retriever. Matt Claussen handled Merlyn.

Disaster dogs must have a high level of obedience, tempered with the ability to work independently

Merlyn and Jenner (below) regularly train on obstacle courses (far left) and man-made rubble piles, so that when they are at a real disaster site, they can safely and confidently navigate the dangerous terrain.

Ann admits that despite all the training and trust she has in her dogs, it is always worrisome when they disappear into the rubble out of her eyesight, even if just for a moment while checking for scent.

Natural disasters:
Tornadoes, floods, hurricanes,
and earthquakes

Although the Oklahoma City bombing and the events of September 11 focused the world's attention on the rescue and recovery roles of disaster dogs, FEMA task forces respond to far more than terrorist attacks. Their most frequent role is responding to natural disasters, such as the tornadoes that devastated Oklahoma in 1999, shown here.

Hurricane Katrina was a challenge for dog handlers

The enormity of the destruction and debris in the aftermath of Hurricane Katrina in 2005 made the search for living (and later dead) victims difficult. In addition to the normal perils of rubble work (sharp objects and unsteady ground among them), the dogs and handlers had to contend with contaminated water, deep mud, stray dogs intent on defending their territory, and the difficult logistics of working in an area where the local infrastructure was destroyed.

AVALANCHE DOGS

Dogs can help pinpoint where avalanche victims are buried under the snow, so rescue workers can quickly recover them

A Swiss study shows that 90 percent of people buried in avalanches survive if they are recovered in the first fifteen minutes. After thirty-five minutes, this rate drops to only 30 percent, and chances for survival after two hours is a mere 3 percent

The science of avalanche forecasting has advanced significantly in recent years, but analysts still cannot predict with exact precision when or where an avalanche will occur. New technology and bolder outdoor enthusiasts are pushing more and more skiers, hikers and snowmobilers into avalanche country. And even on "safe" days, many still fall victim to these forces of nature.

Other information collected in a study by the National Research Council of Canada's Associate Committee on Geotechnical Research found that one well-trained avalanche search dog could cover more ground in thirty minutes than twenty human foot searchers, using the traditional search method of probing poles, could in two hours—implying that the dogs are eighty times more efficient.

The key to success is being able to get the dogs and their handlers to the scene on time.

If the dogs arrive quickly there is hope

Ski Patrol dogs are taught to ride in chairlifts, snowmobiles and helicopters, so that they can quickly get to the scene of an avalanche

The scent of the human body moves through the snow and eventually reaches the surface, where the dog can smell it.

The route of the scent through the snow can meander, so the exact spot the dog alerts may not be precisely above the body, but it is usually close enough to enable human searchers with probing poles to narrow in quickly. Without the dogs, a line of searchers with probes could take hours to find the victim.

The success of the dogs is affected by the snow characteristics of the avalanche, the weather conditions, and the buried depth of the victim. According to statistics compiled by ski patrol K9 handler Kim Gilmore, dogs in Austria have been able to detect bodies that were buried under up to thirty-five feet of snow.

Coup saved a skier buried for ninety minutes under four feet of snow

A rescue helicopter whisked ski patrolman Jerry Balint and his rescue dog, Coup, to the scene of an avalanche near the Jackson Hole Ski Area in Wyoming in 1992. Meanwhile, four feet below the surface, skier Robert Dunlap frantically used his watch as a tool to help carve a small air pocket near his face.

Rescuers had been digging vainly in the snow looking for Dunlap. Immediately after arriving, Balint gave his dog the "Hunt 'em up, Coup" command. It took his black lab only a few seconds to pinpoint the buried skier and begin her digging alert. By the time rescuers extracted Dunlap from his would-be frozen tomb, he had been under the snow for ninety minutes. He limped away with only a torn knee ligament and mild hypothermia. Later, it was estimated he was carried down over nine hundred vertical feet, including drops over sixty-five-foot cliffs.

Coup was inducted into the Wyoming Animal Hall of Fame for her rescue achievements. Sadly, she was killed by a moose less than a year after saving Dunlap.

Keno makes the first live find by an avalanche dog in Canada

Ski patrol dog arrives within minutes to save a skier caught in an avalanche near the Fernie Ski Resort

Ski patrol dog Keno was the hero of Canada in December 2000, when he located a skier who was caught in an avalanche near the Fernie Alpine Resort in British Columbia. This was the first live find in Canada by an avalanche dog.

Ryan Radchenko, a ski lift operator who was enjoying the off-limits slopes of Fernie before the public opening, accidentally triggered an avalanche. The force of the snow carried him four hundred and fifty feet down the mountainside. When the snowy ride stopped, he immediately started to punch his hand toward the surface in a failed effort at self-rescue.

Keno and his ski patrol handler Robin Siggers arrived on the nearby scene within minutes. It didn't take Keno long to catch the scent and start digging furiously until he was twelve inches deep and found Radchenko's outreached hand. The dog pulled off the glove and urgently returned with it to his handler.

All the human rescuers immediately took up the task of digging, and the victim was removed in a state of semi-consciousness after being buried nearly thirty minutes.

Rescuers on the scene agree that without Keno's speedy alert, Radchenko would have died of suffocation before the human searchers could have found him using the traditional method: a line of searchers, each armed with probing poles to check the snow.

Seven Tips for surviving an avalanche

1. **Heed Warnings.** Pay attention to avalanche warnings and learn the danger signs.
2. **Travel in Groups.** Never travel alone, but cross potential avalanche chutes in a single file with significant distance between each person.
3. **Transceivers and Probes.** Carry the right equipment for rescue—an avalanche transceiver, shovel, probe, and a cell phone to call for help.
4. **Swim or Roll.** If you're caught in an avalanche, try to "swim" on the surface or roll out sideways.
5. **Spit.** When buried, you'll be disoriented. Spit to use gravity to figure out which way is up.
6. **Make an Air Pocket.** Dig quickly to create an air pocket to increase your available air.
7. **Remain Calm.** Amazing rescues have occurred, especially when dogs can be flown to the scene quickly.

WATER RECOVERY DOGS

Dogs can help divers locate and recover drowned victims

Recovering a body is a sad task, but an important one to help ease the pain of families who have lost loved ones to drownings

Although these water recovery dogs don't jump in and pull the victim out, they can tell divers where the scent is emanating from the water. In this way, the dogs are able to reduce the search area in a body of water to a few hundred feet, making the job exponentially easier for the divers.

Most water dogs are taught to alert at the point of the strongest scent. Yukon (far right), a German shepherd, will paw and bark at the spot; while Ajax (bottom right), a German shorthaired pointer, prefers to point (no surprise!). The golden retriever (above right) prepares to launch into the water and swim a figure eight over the site. Many different types of alert are acceptable, so long as the dog is consistent and the handler can "read" it.

Well-trained search dogs can detect a body that is two hundred feet deep

Because the current pulls the scent as it rises through the water, the body is not usually directly below where the dog alerts. Instead, the depth of the body, the strength of the current, the temperature of the water, thermoclines, and other factors affect the accuracy of the ID—but the divers can take these factors into account when they go under, and adjust their position accordingly.

Underwater side-scan sonar and other high tech gear has been used to confirm that dogs can detect the scent of a drowning victim at depths up to two hundred feet.

Interestingly, some water dogs have even been used on frozen lakes when "breathing holes" are drilled into the ice for the dogs to scent the water beneath. This is only useful if you have experienced ice divers willing and able to retrieve the victim's body.

Some dogs train with divers, who pop out of the water and reward them with food or play. This is highly motivational for the dogs, helping to get them interested in what is underneath the water, and keeping them excited about the "game"

The "swim alert" is easy to read, because when the dog catches the scent he dives into the water and swims a figure eight above the point of the strongest scent. This can be done by a dog working from shore (such as a river situation) or from a boat.

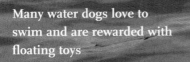

Many water dogs love to swim and are rewarded with floating toys

Water Rescue Dogs

Most water "rescue" dogs are really recovery dogs who help divers locate the bodies of drowned victims under the water. However, Newfoundland dogs have a proud history of true water rescue work, serving as lifeguards searching the coastline for shipwrecked sailors and pulling them to shore.

In 1919, the S.S. *Ethie* was grounded on the dangerous coast of Newfoundland. Accounts from the time purport that a Newfoundland worked ceaselessly to bring over ninety people to shore before drowning from exhaustion. And in the 1930s in England, the famed dog Swansea Jack was credited with twenty-seven rescues.

Today, water rescue is primarily a sport for Newfoundlands. These 150-pound dogs can easily tow a small stranded boat to shore, or pull several people at one time. They often wear a harness that enables the person to grab hold. If the victim is unable to do so, the dog gently grabs the person's wrist in his mouth and pulls them to safety.

EVIDENCE/ARTICLE DOGS

"Article" dogs are trained to find missing or discarded objects that can be used as evidence in criminal cases or to help establish where a lost person travelled

Shotgun shells are just one type of evidence that dogs can easily find

"Trust your dog," is a reccurring refrain from search dog handlers. Several days after a crime, Patti Gibson from ILL-WIS SAR Dogs was given a scent article and asked to use her bloodhound Gracie to seek discarded evidence on the path the suspect took. The dog led her several blocks before giving a sit alert to indicate that the suspect had entered a car. Her police escort then confirmed that this was where they had caught and loaded the man into a squad car.

Almost on a whim, Patti asked her dog to "get 'em again." Gracie raised her head, sniffed the air and dragged her handler seventy-five feet down a ravine into a pool of shallow water. As she lay down in the water, Patti twice scolded the dog to "get back to work," thinking her bloodhound was taking an unscheduled break to cool off.

"She gave me that disgusted hound look, put her head completely under the water and pulled out a hatchet," explained Patti. The police were able to pull a print off the weapon, and this evidence helped in the conviction of the suspect.

Jake, from Arkansas Game and Fish, shows off his prowess at finding evidence by locating a discarded handgun

HUMAN REMAINS

"Cadaver" or human remains detection dogs are taught to find bodies

At first glance, one might ask, "Why would anyone want to train his dog to do that?"

The death of a loved one is a difficult burden for anyone, but when there is no body—no physical proof—that this person is dead, it is even more difficult to find closure. And in the case of a homicide, it makes it exponentially more difficult to convict the murderer.

Cadaver/HRD (Human Remains Detection) dogs are a powerful tool in helping the police locate missing people who are feared dead. They can locate unembalmed bodies that have been buried, or pinpoint minute traces of blood to establish a crime scene.

Cadaver-scented mannequins can be used to give more realistic training

The dog is first introduced to the mannequin while it is playing with a favorite toy (right), to encourage a positive association with it.

Even if dogs are not going to specialize in human remains detection work, they must learn that telling their handlers about finding the remains earns them big rewards.

"When you set out on a search, you never know whether the victim is still alive or if they have perished in the field," explains K9 instructor Jonni Joyce. "Some dogs have an aversion to cadavers, and may carefully and purposefully lead you away from a body unless they are trained otherwise."

Identifying unmarked Civil War graves

Once a dog has been trained to find cadaver material, he can move on to buried remains. It is not unusual for the dog to be able to find old graves on Civil War battlefields or in paupers' fields—as long as the body or bodies are not embalmed, because this prevents the decomposition smells that the dog is trying to find.

Tests comparing ground penetrating radar to the dog's results often show a well-trained dog has more confirmed finds, proving that dogs are a quick, inexpensive and (most importantly) noninvasive way for anthropologists and contractors to find unmarked gravesites.

The current trend is to train a "down" alert when the dog detects human remains

This is instead of an aggressive "dig" alert that could damage potential evidence at a crime scene. It is important to note that this "down" is very easily distinguished from a dog that is simply lying down to rest. Alley, above, demonstrates the very attentive down alert.

Trainers sometimes use cadaver-scented toys (left) to get young pups interested in the "game" of finding human remains.

Most cadaver searches come up empty

According to cadaver dog expert Andrew Rebmann (left with Griz), 94 percent of his speculative cadaver searches turn up negative. This might seem like a lot of "wasted" time, but cadaver dogs are often used to rule out potential murder or burial sites for police. "It's a noninvasive way to check for graves or evidence. People are much more likely to let you run a dog through their backyard than let you start digging," explains his partner Marcia Koenig. "And the court is more likely to approve a dog than a backhoe when asking for a search warrant. We can quickly check out vague leads the police have gotten, and give the homeowners some peace of mind."

Airplane crash sites

Marcia Koenig and Coyote (below) responded to the Crash of KAL Flight 801 in Guam in 1997 as part of FEMA's Puget Sound Urban Search and Rescue (USAR) Task Force. In most air crashes, human searchers are able to recover the obvious victims. However, when small body parts, burned remains, and mud-buried bodies are involved, dogs are the most efficient method for finding them.

Conditions for the search were difficult because it was the middle of the monsoon season. Deep mud made walking difficult for the dogs and handlers, and 90°F temperatures with 100 percent humidity put them at great risk of dehydration. Despite these difficult conditions, the dog teams were able to identify and recover a significant amount of remains missed by other search methods.

Training aids are challenging

One of the more difficult aspects of training cadaver dogs is securing and safely handling the training aids. A wide variety of materials must be used because the body smells differently at various stages of decay. Common aids include blood, tissue at all stages of decay, hair, bones, and teeth (which are the last to disappear).

Synthetic scents called Pseudoscent can also be used, and there are three main types: fresh decomposition, older decomposition, and underwater decomposition. There is also a synthetic "fear" scent, which may be useful in recent homicides.

Teaching the dog to look up

Human remains detection dogs need to learn that the scent they're looking for can be high in the air. This would be the case in a suicide by hanging, or a flood (when waters recede, bodies can remain hooked in the trees). Surprisingly, it can also occur with old graves. The scent of an old burial is often first detected in a nearby tree which exudes the scent through its leaves.

POLICE DOGS

The modern police dog is a mixture of protector, searcher and community hero

Many police dogs live at home with their law enforcement handlers as family pets during off-duty hours
Today's police dogs do far more than act as their partners' enforcers, with a mean bark and meaner bite for the bad guy. The tracking dog can follow the hot trail of a fleeing suspect, and subdue him if necessary. The scent-discriminating search dog can trail a lost or abducted child, or identify a suspect from a scent article. Narcotics dogs can find everything from a marijuana seed on the floor of a car to kilos of heroin tucked into a hidden compartment. Bomb dogs sniff out explosives at airports and train stations, while arson dogs can help investigators by indicating exactly where accelerants were used. Cadaver dogs can find hidden graves. And evidence dogs can locate discarded or hidden weapons, or other incriminating evidence.

Whisky is a hunting dog by day and a narcotics dog by night

Whisky's career started differently than most police dogs'. Dr. Gayla Combes, a veterinarian in Perry, Oklahoma, bought this Deutsch Kurzhaar (German shorthair pointer) as her personal hunting dog. Her husband Mark Combes, a local police officer, watched the dog hunt and decided his capabilities were being "wasted" on quail. He began training the dog for narcotics and soon had him certified.

All is well in the Combes' household until hunting season starts, and the competition for Whisky's expertise begins. Who gets to use the dog today? Community service always wins, but the compromise is that off-duty hours are spent hunting. On more than a few occasions, Sgt. Combes's pager has gone off while hunting, because a fellow officer has stopped a suspicious car.

"It always raises eyebrows when I show up in hunting gear with a mud-covered dog," grins Sgt. Combes. "But Whisky would just as soon be pointing out narcotics as pointing quail."

Police canines often have dual roles. First and foremost, they must protect their human partners, so that the officers can in turn protect the community

Bruno and retired Officer William Proulx of the East Hartford Police Department (Connecticut) personify this. Bruno, now deceased, was a four-time Connecticut Police K9 Olympic winner and an excellent tracker who had followed and apprehended many suspects. However, he is best remembered by his handler as the dog who saved his life on more than one occasion.

A case in point was a "routine" traffic stop not unlike the one pictured here. The driver became aggressive. When Officer Proulx reached in to remove the keys from the ignition, the driver floored the engine dragging the policeman alongside the car.

Bruno, trained to watch out of the front seat window and self-deploy if he spotted danger, did just that. "The next thing I knew, Bruno was in the front seat of the car, and the man wisely came to an abrupt halt," recounts Officer Proulx.

Bruno acts as a deterrent by standing at-the-ready should his police handler need his help

Police dogs must be bold and
possess excellent physical prowess

Police search and detection dogs help catch criminals and increase the rate of convictions

For hundreds of years, the law has used man-tracking dogs to catch fleeing criminals. However, there are more subtle ways that "scent evidence" can help the police:

1. Unable to follow a trail to its conclusion, a dog may at least be able to determine a suspect's direction of travel, thereby narrowing down the search area.

2. Days after the crime, a dog can link a crime scene to a suspect by establishing a scent trail to a place the suspect is known to have been (such as his home).

3. A dog can locate discarded or hidden evidence.

4. Dogs can identify a suspect in a crowd. If a car thief were to abandon a stolen vehicle and run into a crowded bar to hide, the dog could be scented off the driver's seat and then "tag" the person who matched the scent.

5. Using a police lineup, dogs can pick out the suspect that matches the scent on a piece of evidence.

6. Dogs can be used to produce probable cause for a search. A typical example is the narcotics dog who indicates the presence of drugs in a car.

Mighty Mony: an airport's guardian angel

Det. Jonni Joyce patrols the parking lots, baggage areas, tarmac, and far corners of the airport with Mighty Mony, her canine partner. This friendly yellow lab is part of the Raleigh-Durham Airport Police Department's Explosive Detection Canine Unit.

Mony was hours away from euthanasia at a shelter when her potential as a working dog was recognized. "She has extraordinary scenting capabilities and an incredible desire to work," explains her initial trainer, Christopher Weeks, a former Marine Corps dog instructor.

Mony is able to find the slightest traces of any number of explosives or their components, even when sealed in plastic, placed in closed containers, sewn into the lining of suitcases, or hidden in countless other clever manners.

Bomb patrol is a team effort, however. "My job is to think like a terrorist, so I can put my dog in the places that explosives might be hidden," explains Det. Joyce. "If they're there, she'll find them."

Mighty Mony was named in honor of slain police officer Lt. Monica Carey of the Clayton, North Carolina Police Department

On September 14, 2001, while the country was still focused on the aftermath of the terrorist attacks on the World Trade Center and the Pentagon, Lt. Carey was killed in the line of duty while fighting the local war on drugs on the streets of this small American town. She left behind two children and a husband.

MILITARY DOGS

More than just patrol dogs, U.S. military canines perform some spectacular feats

The First Marine Dog Platoon (below) was used to secure the beachhead at Bougainville (Solomon Islands) during WWII. The all–Doberman pinscher platoon had twelve scout dogs, six sentry (guard) dogs, three messenger dogs, and three dogs that searched for the wounded. The tradition continues with today's military using dogs in a variety of ways.

U.S. Navy dog Rocky disarms a soldier during a drill, while his handler covers from a safe distance

Explosive ordnance and landmine detection dogs

U.S. Army SGG Richard Price and his military working dog, Dick, investigate an explosion site in Gayevi, Bosnia-Herzegovina. The dog is trained to detect the smell of explosive components.

Although the U.S. military does not currently train landmine dogs, many other countries and private organizations use such dogs to help detect landmines so that they can be safely dismantled.

Bomb detector

Cassie, a two-year-old yellow Labrador retriever, poses among inert examples of the kinds of explosives she is trained to find at the Lackland Air Force Base. Lackland is the the home of the famed Defense Department Military Working Dog (MWD) School, which trains all of the armed services dogs. Cassie is being trained for a career in bomb detection.

Sentry/guard dogs

In addition to their roles as scout and explosive detection dogs, most modern military dogs are also trained to guard and aggressively protect their handlers and fellow soldiers, or apprehend and subdue dangerous persons.

Draft dogs

Historically, many countries used military dogs as draft animals to pull machine guns, supply carts (below), or ambulance stretchers. The U.S. used sled dogs in Alaska and Greenland.

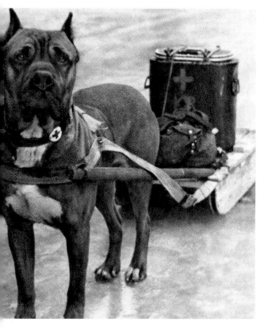

Air Force dogs patrol the bases
and check aircraft for sabotage

Andy, the Doberman marine

Andy the scout dog and his handler PFC Robert E. Lansley (right) were with the Marine Raider Regiment at Bougainville (Solomon Islands) during WWII.

Unlike sentry dogs that remained at camp as guards, the scouts went out ahead of troops to look for trouble. While most scout dogs worked on leash, Andy was so dependable he worked off-lead about twenty-five yards in front of the company, alerting the marines to the presence of danger ahead. He is accredited with saving many lives by helping them avoid Japanese ambushes. His full story can be found in *Dogs at War* by Clayton G. Going (1944, Macmillan Co.).

Detection dogs regularly check cargo, baggage and vehicles on the bases for drugs, firearms or explosives

Because the handler's life, and those of his comrades, can depend upon the performance of the dog, military handlers develop exceptionally strong bonds with their canine partners. At left, a handler roughhouses with his dog after completing a training exercise. A sentimental French postcard (far left, circa 1919) shows an ambulance dog mourning the loss of its handler

U.S. CUSTOMS & THE ATF

Imagine a dog who can detect currency by the scent of the inks or indicate if an accelerant was used to start a suspicious fire

You'd be picturing the dogs of the U.S. Customs and the Bureau of Alcohol, Tobacco and Firearms.
These two agencies work together to train elite law enforcement detection dogs. Currency dogs are just one of the canine detection specialists employed by the U.S.

Customs. They are trained to detect the special inks used exclusively in U.S. paper money, and are the front line of defense against money laundering schemes. In 2000 they seized $29.4 million in cash being sneaked across the border.

A dog runs the "treadmill" to check packages as they go by

U.S. Customs has started an internal breeding program at the Virginia training center. The goal is to develop dogs ideally suited for detection work, and to have more control over their early stages of development and training

The Customs/ATF joint training school teaches handlers all aspects of working with dogs, from grooming and health, to actual search training

The Customs/ATF Canine Enforcement Training Center in Front Royal, Virginia, is one of the most advanced dog and handler schools in the world. Like a university, human and canine students study for different majors, such as the ATF's Accelerant and Explosives Detection Dog program, or the Customs Narcotic Detection Dog program.

"We've come a long way since training our first arson dog in 1986," said facility director Bradley A. Buckles. The training center occupies 250 acres and accommodates 260 dogs in training.

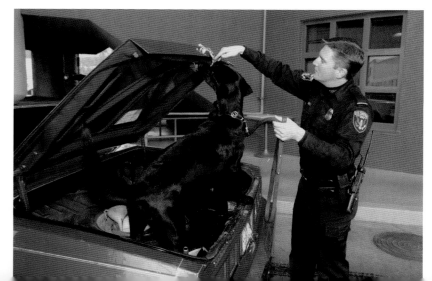

The ATF trains many of the nation's arson dogs

Fire departments, law enforcement agencies, and even insurance companies all know that arson dogs are important tools in fire investigation, because they can quickly determine if accelerants like gasoline, paint thinner, kerosene, and alcohol were used and pinpoint where, so that investigators can collect and analyze evidence.

Identifying 1/1000th of a drop of 50 percent evaporated gasoline is an easy task for a well-trained arson dog. On a normal training day, an ATF dog does 125 repetitions of detecting accelerants—that's 45,000 training sessions a year!

Customs dogs made 11,506 drug and currency detections in 2000, resulting in 6476 arrests

Customs dogs can be found at ports of entry where people or packages come into the country. They can work on a moving treadmill (upper left), check airport baggage and passengers (center left), and suspicious vehicles (bottom left).

Customs narcotics dogs are trained to aggressively dig at drugs—this dog shows where they have been hidden in a wall (right).

U.S. DEPT. OF AGRICULTURE

The USDA's "Beagle Brigade" sniffs out food and plants that are smuggled across the border

These products can harbor pests and diseases that have the potential to devastate American crops, wildlife, or wilderness

Texanna ("Tex"), a beagle rescued from an animal control facility in Houston, Texas, has done it all with the United States Department of Agriculture (USDA) as part of their Animal and Plant Health Inspection Service's heralded "Beagle Brigade." She and K9 handler Wendy Beltz have worked airports, seaports, postal cargo depots, and land borders looking for contraband agricultural products that are accidentally or purposely smuggled across the border.

Like other dogs in the program, "Tex" is trained to alert on over one hundred odors, including apple, citrus, meat, pear, mango, and more. Additionally, she is trained to ignore nontargets, such as cheese. Most USDA dogs do a "sit" alert to inform the handler that they have found one of the "target" items. Tex, always the showgirl, usually chooses to add a victory howl (far right) to her trained alert! This invariably brings cheers from spectators watching her work.

The USDA's canine program is extremely efficient. In 2001, these dogs screened over 42,000 airplane flights and 8.6 million passengers, making over 55,000 seizures. Additionally, over 20,000 vehicles were checked at land borders with almost 4000 seizures.

"Sometimes people simply forget they have fruits in their bag, but often it's purposeful smuggling by someone trying to bring a gift," explains Eastern Regional Coordinator Alison E. Pae. "They simply don't realize the incredible danger that one piece of fruit could harbor."

"Mothers get blamed for everything." adds Wendy Beltz. " 'Oh, my mom packed it' has to be the most common excuse we hear."

Tex shows off her best beagle howl, which she uses (along with a sit) to alert her handler that she has found contraband

Guam's fight against brown tree snakes

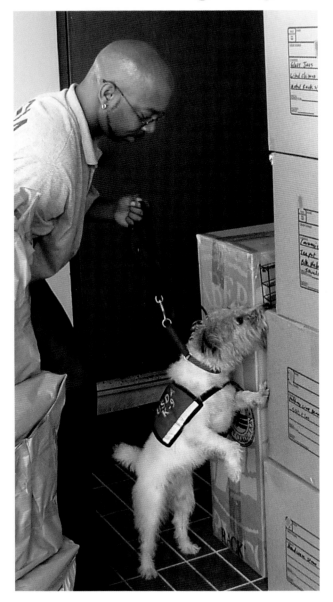

These non-native snakes have overtaken this island, causing the extinction of most of the native forest birds, wreaking havoc on the economy and causing islandwide power failures

The trouble most likely started when a female brown tree snake hitched a ride on a U.S. military plane after World War II. With no native predators and an abundant supply of helpless birds, the snakes exploded in population. Now there are between 5,000 to 10,000 snakes per square mile on Guam, Micronesia.

Now nine out of twelve of the native species of forest birds are already extinct on the island, and the three remaining species are on the endangered list. "The native birds simply had no natural defenses against these voracious snakes," explains Daniel Vice, assistant state director of the United States Department of Agriculture (USDA) Wildlife Services in Guam.

These five-foot snakes also have an annoying habit of climbing the power lines and electrocuting themselves, often causing local and islandwide power outages.

The brown tree snake is a nocturnal hunter attracted to dark, cool places like cargo warehouses, ship holds, or airplane cargo bays, which leads to a serious risk of accidental exportation. Because of this preference and their agile climbing ability, there is the extreme threat that they will accidentally be exported to Hawaii, the Mariana Islands, or other places susceptible to a similar snake infestation.

In 1993 the USDA initiated a K9 program to attack this threat. Their cadre of Jack Russell terriers are the last line of defense, checking cargo warehouses, planes, and ships leaving Guam for susceptible areas.

"DNA tests suggest that the entire population of brown tree snakes in Guam descend from one female that slipped in after WW2. That's why it's so critical that we catch every snake before they make it to Hawaii," explains the USDA

WILDLIFE ENFORCEMENT

Many national parks and state fish and game commissions use dogs for wildlife enforcement, patrol, search and rescue, and environmental protection.

America's state and national parks and reserves are policed by the National Park Service, state fish and game, or environmental police departments—some of which have canine programs.

The state of Arkansas began a canine program in 1999, modeling it after the Florida Fish and Wildlife Conservation's initial successful program. Lt. Christopher Carpenter and his chocolate Labrador retriever Jake (left), Cpl. Frankie Tucker and his black Labrador retriever Doc (right), and Sgt. Emery and Moose (not shown) have myriad responsibilities. The dogs can track lawbreakers or lost citizens, detect potentially poached meats such as venison, duck and turkey, and recover evidence such as guns.

Although this is a young program, by early 2002 the Arkansas dog teams had already been responsible for over two hundred Game and Fish arrests (such as illegal wildlife baiting or hunting violations), and have assisted other law enforcement agencies in several dozen arrests, including felonies.

Jake's career as a wildlife dog (left) began at the age of 2½ years when his owners were killed in a double homicide. He was placed in a shelter before being rescued and trained for the program.

Comanche guards our national parks from poachers and other criminals

Catching poachers is just one of Comanche's many jobs in Grand Teton National Park. He and his handler, Ranger Janet Wilts, also perform search and rescue missions, locate drugs being transported through the park, and find evidence of crimes.

They are even called into action to find buried paragliding chutes after thrill-seekers make illegal jumps from the Tetons. This dangerous stunt could likely lead to a rescue mission that puts many people's lives at stake. These law-breakers try to conceal their crimes by burying their chutes and then pretending to be normal hikers leaving the scene. They then return at a safer time to retrieve their chutes—unless Comanche gets there first!

Antlers are a crucial part of the food chain, so their theft can be devastating to local animal species

Antlers are used in taxidermy and coveted as souvenirs, so criminals are tempted to abscond with them from national parks and recreation areas. Even though the elk and deer shed their antlers naturally each year, their removal can wreak havoc on the local ecosystem because they contain calcium and minerals that are crucial to the survival of the many species of animals that consume them.

Comanche is trained to point out antlers to his National Parks System handler Janet Wilts. He is trained to find large caches that thieves have hidden near the road for easy collection. This allows the rangers to set up a stakeout and nab the offenders when they return. In much the same way he finds narcotics, Comanche can detect an individual antler that a tourist has carefully hidden in a car.

Enforcement K9s from the Arkansas Game and Fish Commission can track lost persons, find poached game meats, or search out hidden and discarded evidence like firearms. Doc (right) locates venison in a cooler, while Jake searches for spent shell casings (below) and drugs (bottom right)

Worried about termites, cancer, gas leaks, or a lost pet? A number of new specialty detector dogs can help find all sorts of potential problems

Specially trained termite dogs can give a home a much more thorough check than visual inspection alone

Termite hunting dogs are becoming more and more popular with home inspectors. Humans can only look for telltale visual signs of infestation, but dogs can be trained to smell termites inside the walls and under the crawl spaces where visual inspection is not always possible.

Beagles are a popular choice for termite dogs because of their small size and friendly nature. They were originally bred to hunt rabbits, so it is not that big of a leap to change their quarry to termites. It just takes the proper training, with big rewards for finding termites. Although beagles currently dominate the canine termite business, many different breeds (or mixed breeds) can be used.

Dogs can be taught to check for some types of cancer with greater accuracy than doctors

In the 1980s and 1990s several doctors in England and the United States did studies in which dogs were taught to identify skin cancer by the different smell of cancerous cells. First, a dog was taught to detect known samples of cancer in a petri dish, and then moved on to live subjects. In one Florida study by Dr. Cognetta, a standard schnauzer named George was trained to accurately point out melanoma in its early stages. George proved to have 99% accuracy on lab samples, and identified the disease in six out of seven people in a test on live subjects.

Until recently, this new area of detection never left the research labs. Now there are several dogs being trained for cancer detection in the United States. Shing Ling is a standard poodle being employed by the Pine Street Chinese Benevolent Association, an acupuncture center in California. For her training, she smells the patient's exhaled breath to detect lung and other types of cancer. One advantage to this approach is that samples of a person's exhaled breath can be "bagged" and the dog can check them remotely. At press time, clinical studies of her success rates were not yet available, but the results look promising for this new area.

A dog is also being trained for a doctor in Michigan, with hopes that he will become the first cancer dog in private medical practice.

Real-life "Ace Ventura" pet detectives

It's not hard to imagine the panic you might feel if your pet disappears. A tracking dog might be able to help

A few industrious dog handlers have taken their experiences in scent-discrimination, and started training pet-tracking dogs. "Rachel just loves cats," explains Kathy "Kat" Albrecht, a retired police K9 handler. "You can't imagine her expression when one day I handed her a scent article from a kitten, and said 'Go find.' After years of telling her not to chase them, she thought it was Christmas morning!"

It's not just cats that can be followed. If the dog is trained to scent-discriminate, it can just as easily follow a dog, ferret, or snake.

Kat has recently turned her PetHunter business into the not-for-profit Lost-A-Pet foundation. Her dream is to create local agencies around the country that will help pet owners reunite with their lost animals.

Gas and Oil Leaks
A few gas and oil companies have used dogs to quickly pinpoint the source of costly and dangerous leaks. A chemical called Tekscent can be added to a pipeline. Dogs can smell this chemical and thereby locate the leaks.

Mercury Cleanup
Sweden's Environmental Protection Agency has used dogs in recent years to locate hidden mercury contamination in the nation's schools. They were shocked to find much higher amounts than expected, with the dogs locating mercury on shelves, in sinks and in floor crevices.

Truffle Hunters
Move over swine! Instead of pigs, truffle hunting dogs are now being increasingly employed by Italian truffle hunters. Wild truffle hunting is a secretive business, usually done at night with dark-colored dogs to keep favorite truffle grounds hidden from competitors.

GETTING STARTED

Hundreds of people in the United States do volunteer canine search and rescue. Here's some tips on getting started

1 Do you have the time and finances to participate in this volunteer activity?

Volunteer canine search and rescue is incredibly time consuming, and can be very expensive as well. Most volunteers spend between four hundred and five hundred hours a year (that's ten hours a week) in training activities. An experienced handler can usually train a new dog in six months to two years, depending on the specialty. It can take beginner handlers much longer, and their first dog might be "washed out" of the program.

Most estimate that their expenses (training, equipment, mileage, vet bills, and more) are at least $2000 a year, with many spending well over $5000 of their own money.

2 Join a respectable search unit

The best place to start is with your local canine or general search unit. Not only is this a good place to learn dog handling skills, but you'll also learn important things like general search and rescue techniques, incident command structure, professionalism, and search procedures and protocols.

If the unit is also a registered not-for-profit organization, then your canine training expenses may be tax deductible.

See page 126 for a list of websites with databases of SAR units.

3 Train, train, and train some more

Most dogs progress quickly if they are trained several times a week. The majority of the canine units train weekly as a group, and members are expected to train on their own midweek. Even after a dog has been certified, it must continue its training or it will lose its edge. This is not an activity where you can rest on your laurels and still be a responsible member of the search community.

4 What if your current dog isn't "search material"?

Are you willing to get another? Your dog might be a show champion, an obedience whiz, the king of tennis balls, or otherwise "perfect," yet he still may not have that mix of traits that makes for a great search dog. Once you take on the role of search and rescue, it is your obligation to give the victim the very best. And if your dog doesn't have what it takes, are you willing to "retire" him or her and start training another?

5 They're working dogs first, pets second

You owe it to the victim to field the best dog you can. That means that everything you do with your dog must first meet search dog training criteria. For example, many water recovery dogs associate boats with "work." If you were to take this dog on a family boat ride, you might accidentally ruin his water recovery training, because he might not understand that he wasn't working, and get frustrated.

6 Search and Rescue is more than just dogs

You may have the best trained dog in the world, but you're not much use to your team if you become injured, get lost, or can't tell the search commander precisely where you have searched during your time in the field. In addition to navigation and survival skills, you need to understand the Incident Command System, your unit's role in the search, and your personal responsibilities.

8 The work is often inconvenient and uncomfortable

Searches always seem to be needed in the worst possible weather and conditions and at the most inconvenient times. However, once you make the commitment to canine search and rescue, you can't say no just because a search doesn't meet your schedule. When your beeper goes off, your work, play, sleep and family activities must be abandoned so you can immediately heed the call.

9 Study with the best, share ideas

A common saying in the SAR community is: "If anyone tells you they know everything they need to know about a subject— run!" No matter how much experience and knowledge you have, you can always learn more. Search techniques and dog training methods are constantly being changed and improved. Attend seminars and conferences, and listen and share ideas whenever possible.

7 Set standards and meet them

Most units offer certifications, which are the very minimum standards you must meet before you can be deployed in the field. There are also independent certifications you can obtain from various associations and trainers. You owe it to the victims and their families to keep improving, keep learning and training. Dogs (and their handlers) soon lose their valuable skills if they don't practice them at least on a weekly basis.

10 Do you enjoy the work?

Search and rescue is serious business, but if you don't get some enjoyment out of the training, you won't be able to sustain the effort over hundreds of hours of hard work. In addition, search dogs need to think that search and rescue is the best game in the world, so you must enjoy the training yourself to keep it fun for the dog.

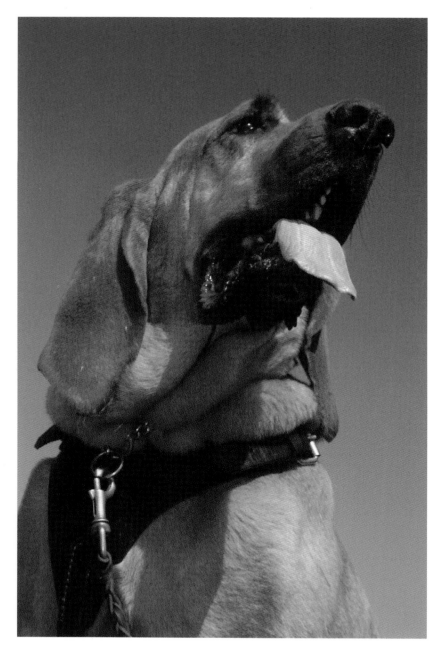

Learn lost person behavior

Lost person behavior characteristics are important for search planners to know. Once the type of victim you are looking for is known, you can use these statistics to help predict where and how to conduct the search.

For example, while most lost adults will actively seek help, children often do not answer searchers' calls—the youngest perhaps because they have been taught to be wary of strangers, and older ones because they may be afraid they will be punished for getting lost.

Alzheimer's patients and despondent people rarely answer calls and may even run or consciously hide from searchers.

Children and Alzheimer's patients are also at the highest risk because their age makes them vulnerable, they usually possess no survival skills, and they are probably not dressed for the weather.

Lost hunters are usually prepared for surviving a longer stay in the outdoors, but they tend to be deeper in the wilderness when they become lost. Their attempts to navigate out often put them further away from searchers.

Many search units have mentioned an increase in calls to find lost Alzheimer's patients, which is not surprising given the numbers published by the Alzheimer's Association. They estimate that four million Americans currently suffer from the disease, including half the population over eighty-five years old. It is therefore wise for search teams to familiarize themselves with patient behavior characteristics.

Many handlers start "training" their dogs at eight weeks old with "puppy games" that mimic the more complex search and detection problems they'll face as adults

Some trainers want a dog that is crazy about ball play

Some search dog trainers will tell you that a dog that loves to play ball has a lot of "prey drive." Because search and detection work is basically "hunting," this drive can be converted to the handler's "prey" of choice—narcotics, lost persons, brown tree snakes, etc. It also gives the trainer an easy reward system: "Do your job and you get this ball!" However, many great search dogs have no interest in balls, and many ball-crazy dogs have no interest in search!

Other traits that often yield a good search dog include high energy and focus (as opposed to hyperactivity without focus), sociability, trainability, intelligence, independence, and exceptional athleticism.

The breed of the dog is not as important as his desire to work

Many of the best search dogs have been mixed breeds rescued from the brink of euthanasia

Flipping through this book it becomes obvious that many different breeds of dogs (as well as mixed-breed mutts) are represented among the ranks of search dogs. Many trainers have a favorite breed, but most will agree that it is the traits and drives of the individual dog and his training that count the most.

A great many search and detection dogs get their start after being rescued from shelters. Often these dogs have been turned in or abandoned because they have a high energy level, which can lead to destructive tendencies if the dog doesn't get enough exercise. However, when this energy is channeled into a constructive activity like search work, one often ends up with an exceptional working dog.

The "runaway" is a popular way to start a new search dog

A The "victim" entices the dog into wanting to play or receive a reward

Usually, during the first session, someone holds the dog for the handler, and the handler is the "victim" because the dog is highly motivated to play with and find him. This quickly progresses to using family and friends as victims. Once the dog is "invested" in the game, training moves on to strangers.

B The "victim" turns and runs away from the dog to an easy, nearby hiding place

This dash ignites the dog's prey drive, and he immediately wants to chase and catch the runner. If he is an air-scent dog, the victim runs into the wind, so the dog can smell the scent coming from the hiding place. For the trailing or tracking dog, the victim should have the wind at his back, so the dog can only smell the scent from the trail, and not the scent coming from the hiding place.

C Hold the dog back
Build excitement by holding the dog back. Use a flat collar so as not to accidentally punish the dog.

D Release the dog
Timing is everything: Release the dog at the height of excitement, before he loses interest in the game.

E Big rewards!
The reward must be intense and immediate—play, praise, and food or toy—so the dog starts to associate searching for people with fun, fun, fun!

Suggested Reading

Cadaver Dog Handbook: Forensic Training and Tactics for the Recovery of Human Remains
by Andrew J. Rebmann, Marcia Koenig, Edward David, Marcella H. Sorg
The name says it all. This book covers all types of cadaver searches, including how to search, training materials, and professional considerations.

The Culture Clash
by Jean Donaldson
This book teaches you about your dog's thought processes (stripped of all the Hollywood emotions we often attribute to them), so that you can improve your training methods. Winner of the Maxwell Best Training Book Award.

Death, Daring and Disaster:
Search and Rescue in the National Parks
by Charles R. Butch Farabee
375 exciting tales of heroism and tragedy are drawn from SAR missions carried out by the National Park Service since Yellowstone National Park was established in 1872—a few using search and rescue dogs.

Don't Shoot the Dog :
The New Art of Teaching and Training
by Karen Pryor
Positive (operant) training at its best. If you haven't read the book, do so before you start training your dog. Whether you decide to use a clicker or not, this book is all about timing and shaping behavior to achieve your training goals.

Educational Websites

Avalanche Dogs
www.comdens.com/SAR
Avalanche and general K9 SAR training information

Beaufort Wind Scale
http://sln.fi.edu/tfi/units/ energy/table1.html/
An important tool for judging wind conditions

Cadaver Dogs
www.cadaverdog.com
Site from the authors of the *Cadaver Dog Handbook*

The Crime Library
www.crimelibrary.com/ forensics/k9
Cadaver dog information

FEMA Canine Standards
www.fema.gov/usr/ usr_canines.shtm
Standards for FEMA Disaster Dog certification

How SAR dogs work
http://travel.howstuffworks.com/sar-dog5.htm
Learn how search and rescue dogs work

Idaho Mountain SAR
www.imsaru.org
Click on the "education" link for outdoor safety tips

Jonni Joyce Seminars
www.jonnijoyce.com
Training articles on SAR, police dogs, leadership, and a code of ethics paper

Lost Person Statistics
www.sarbc.org/behchar.html
Lost person behavior, compiled by the SAR Society of British Columbia

NAPWDA
www.napwda.com
Training tips from the North American Police Working Dog Association

Nat'l Bloodhound Training
www.bloodhoundtraining.com
Free training downloads

National Narcotic Detector Dog Association
www.nndda.org
Offers online library

On the Trail!
by Jan Tweedie
A basic text on starting a scent-specific trailing dog. Though primarily geared to the working bloodhound, this book can be used by other dog breed handlers as well.

Police Dog Tactics
by Sandy Bryson
Bryson covers all aspects of "the friendly force"—the police dog—including the apprehension of suspects, foot pursuits, building searches, suspect tracking, and detection work of all types.

Ready! The Training of the Search and Rescue Dog
by Susan Bulanda
A comprehensive book on the training of search and rescue dogs.

Scent and the Scenting Dog
by William Syrotuck
Regardless of what type of search dog you plan to train, this is the leading text for understanding scent theory, including how to analyze and understand the "scent picture."

Search and Rescue Dogs
by the American Rescue Dog Association
This guide emphasizes handler and unit training and conditioning for dogs, and covers searches and terrain analysis. Originally oriented toward German shepherds, it has been recently revised to include all breeds.

NASAR
http://www.nasar.org/nasar/sar_dog_fact_sheet.php
SAR dog fact sheet

SAR-Dogs Network
http://www.sar-dogs.com/
Great resource for SAR news

SAR Info
http://www.sarinfo.bc.ca/
Information on the search and rescue community

SearchK9.net
www.searchK9.net/pages/educational.htm
Several good training tips

Shuler Mantrailing
www.jackshuler.com
Training articles for bloodhounds and other breeds

US Police Canine Association
www.uspcak9.com
Medical and training articles

Working Dogs Veterinary Ctr.
www.workingdogs.com/vetboard/UltraBoard.cgi
Working dog medical subjects

K9 Search Gear

Auroralites
www.auroralites.com
Lighted collars and straps for high visibility at night

Canine Clothier
www.ccdogduds.com
Canine search vests and other gear

NASAR
www.nasar.org
Books and videos

Ruffian Specialties
www.ruffianspecialties.com
Search vests

SAR Camp
www.sarcamp.com
K9 rescue gear and more

Schaaf Saddlery
www.schaafleatherwork.com
Traditional leather tracking harnesses

Search Vests
http://www.ccdogduds.com/
Great resource for service dog equipment

Sigma-Aldrich Corporation
www.sigmaaldrich.com
The makers of Pseudoscent artificial corpse scent. Difficult site to navigate, so do a product number search on P7184, P4304, P1310 and P3929

Sit-Stay.com
www.sitstay.com
Dog vests

Finding a Unit

SAR Contacts
www.sarcontacts.org
Searchable list of search units. Includes their websites where applicable

NASAR
www.NASAR.org
The National Association of Search and Rescue maintains a list of member canine and other SAR units

SARONE Database
www.sarone.org
Searchable database of U.S. search units. Check by state or specialty

History and Related Sites

Avalanche Dogs
http://www.comdens.com/SAR/
Resource for avalanche dog training

Dogs of War History
http://community-2.webtv.net/Hahn-50thAP-K9/K9History/index.html
Extensive history of war dogs

Ill-Wis Search Dogs
http://www.illwissardogs.org
Learn about the Illinois-Wisconsin Search & Rescue Dog unit

Vietnam Dog Handler Assoc.
www.vdhaonline.org
Stories, photos, and information on the role of dogs

Whole Dog Journal
http://www.whole-dog-journal.com/
A guide to natural dog care and training

Working K9 Memorials
www.k9memorialcards.com
The stories of police and other working dog heroes who have passed on

Just for Kids

ATF Kids' Page
www.atf.treas.gov/kids/canines.htm
Learn about how the Bureau of Alcohol, Tobacco and Firearms uses working dogs

FBI Kids' Page
www.fbi.gov/kids/dogs/doghome.htm
Lots of fun, child-oriented information on FBI dogs

FEMA for Kids
www.fema.gov/kids/
Canine heroes trading cards that you can print out at home

GLOSSARY

Alert: Defined differently across the country. In this book it refers to a specially trained and unmistakable signal by a dog to indicate to a handler that the subject (or object) of the search has been found.

Ambulance dog: A WWI term for a search dog who checked the battlefield for wounded soldiers. Also called a "Mercy," "Casualty", or "Red Cross" dog.

ATF: The Bureau of Alcohol, Tobacco and Firearms.

Air-scenting dog: A type of search dog who searches for the scent coming off a person. Usually worked off-lead.

Article dog: See evidence dog.

Bark-and-hold: A type of alert where the dog barks continuously for at least thirty seconds to communicate the find.

Bark alert: A type of alert in which the dog barks at the handler to communicate the find.

Body bang: A type of alert in which the dog jumps up and tags the handler to communicate the find.

Bringsel: A special collar that has a stick attached to it. When the dog wants to communicate to the handler

that he has found the subject, he picks the stick up into his mouth.

Cadaster dog: A cadaver dog that specializes in disaster.

Cadaver dog: A type of search dog used to find human remains. Sometimes called a Human Remains Detection (HRD) dog.

Casualty dog: See ambulance dog.

Certification: A standard set by a local or national body. It is usually the minimum standard a dog/handler team must meet in order to be deployed in a real search.

Chimneying: A type of localized air current that pulls the scent straight up, and drops it down at a distance away.

Cold trail: A scent trail that is no longer fresh (the person traveled the path hours or days earlier).

Disaster dog: A dog specially trained to work at disasters, including collapsed buildings. The FEMA-certified disaster dog is trained to only alert on live victims.

Down alert: The dog performs a "down" while making eye contact with

the handler, to indicate that he has found the object of the search.

Evidence dog: A type of search dog who searches for inanimate objects. Often they do scent-specific work, looking for objects with a certain person's scent (such as discarded evidence from a crime). Also called an "article dog."

FEMA: The Federal Emergency Management Agency.

Gridding: A technique used by handlers to systematically cover a large search area in a grid pattern.

Hot trail: A scent trail that is fresh because it is recent.

Human Remains Detection Dog: See cadaver dog.

Incident Command System (ICS): A widely accepted organizational structure for the management of a search. It is led by the Incident Commander or an Incident Command team.

K9: A common abbreviation for canine or dog.

Lead: A long leash.

Mercy dog: See ambulance dog.

Off-lead: A dog who is not attached to the handler with a leash. This type of dog works independently and is usually controlled through voice commands.

On-lead: A dog who works with a long leash that is usually attached to a nonrestrictive harness. Trailing dogs often use leads from ten to thirty feet long.

Ordnance: Weaponry and explosives.

Recovery: Finding or retrieving deceased victims.

Red Cross dog: See ambulance dog.

Refind: When an off-lead search dog finds a search object, he might be at a great distance from the handler. The dog goes back to the handler, and then brings him or her back (refinds) the subject.

Rescue: Finding and aiding live victims.

Scent article: An item that has the subject's scent on it, such as a piece of clothing. Handlers can make a scent article by laying sterile gauze on something the subject has touched, such as a car seat.

Scent cone: When wind hits a victim, it carries the person's scent with it. As this scent disperses it widens out creating a cone-shaped area of scent.

Scent-discrimination: The ability of the dog to follow/find the particular scent the handler asks the dog to follow/find.

Scent pool: Anywhere that scent from a subject collects is called a scent pool.

Sentry dog: A military scout dog that moves forward to seek out ambushes.

SAR: An abbreviation for search and rescue. Usually refers to the general search community, including canine units, or to the activity of searching and rescuing.

Tracking: A type of search in which the dog follows from footstep to footstep.

Trailing: A type of search in which the dog follows the scent trail left by a person who passed through an area. The dog does not necessarily follow the exact path of the person, but rather goes where the scent has landed.

USAR: An abbreviation for the Federal Emergency Management Agency's Urban Search and Rescue task forces. There are currently twenty-seven regional USAR task forces, which address natural and man-made disasters.

USDA: United States Department of Agriculture.

Water recovery dog: A search dog who detects the location of drowned victims under the water, so that divers can retrieve the body.

Wilderness dog: A search dog who primarily searches in a wilderness environment. It usually refers to a dog who works off-lead.

Wildlife dog: Usually refers to a National Parks Department or Environmental Police dog who enforces fish and game laws.

Working dog: A dog who has a service job, such as a dog who works for police, search and rescue, protection, guidance for the blind, etc.

PHOTO CAPTIONS & CREDITS

 PAGE iv: Jack Shuler's bloodhounds (Phoebe, Bull and Killian) at Shuler Kennels in Salem, Illinois. Photo © Jen Bidner.

PAGE vi: Panda jumps a log during wilderness air-scent training with handler Marci Larson at a Jonni Joyce Seminar. Photo © Jen Bidner.

 PAGE 2: An old photograph of a St. Bernard rescue dog and monk on an alpine pass. The most famous St. Bernard was Barry (circa 1800).

 PAGE 2: USAF SSgt. John Smithhart and Rex check a car trunk for explosives. Photo © USAF MSgt. John E. Laskey.

 PAGE 3: German shepherd and Belgian shepherd ambulance dogs. Painting by Louis Agassiz Fuertes, 1919.

 PAGE 4: "Wounded in its Country's Cause." A veterinarian treats a French ambulance dog. From the *Illustrated London News*, 1916.

 PAGE 5: A French "chien sanitaire" postcard (circa 1915–1919) depicting an ambulance dog handler sending one out to search.

 PAGE 5: A German postcard (circa 1915–1919) showing an ambulance dog after he finds a wounded soldier on a snowy battlefield.

PAGE 5: A British ambulance dog (circa 1919) finds a wounded soldier on the battlefield. Probably trained by Col. E.H. Richardson.

PAGES 4–10: Unidentified original photographs of ambulance and war dogs, circa 1915–1919. The ambulance truck and desert photos are American; the others are of European origin.

  PAGES 6–13: These nine images can be found in Col. Richardson's books *War, Police & Watch Dogs* (Wm. Blackwood & Sons, London, 1910); *Watch Dogs* (Hutchinson, London, 1923); and *40 Years with Dogs* (Hutchinson, London, 1923). The images with bloodhounds depict Richardson.

 **PAGE 5:** A German postcard (circa 1915–1919) showing an ambulance dog bringing back a wounded soldier's hat to the handlers.

PAGE 7: A Russian ambulance dog being given a search command by his handler.

 PAGE 7: The cover of *Renni the Rescuer: A Dog of the Battlefield*, by Felix Salten, the author of *Bambi*. (The Sun Dial Press, 1942).

 PAGE 7: Some "Red Cross" dogs were used for public relations and collection. An illustration of a war dog collecting donations.

 PAGE 8: Mark, a messenger dog, being prepared for work in WWII. This dog was given to the British by the French. British Official Photo.

 PAGE 9: An original photograph of European military dogs, handlers and civilians in urban rubble, looking for survivors.

 PAGE 10: Quartermaster War Dog platoon dogs were used on Biak Island, New Guinea to track down hidden Japanese, July 18, 1944.

 PAGE 11: A Gilbert Gaul painting reproduced in the *Ladies' Home Journal*, 1918, depicts Red Cross dogs checking a battlefield at night.

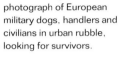 **PAGE 11:** PFC Rez Hester, 7th War Dog Platoon, 25th Regt. naps while Butch stands guard. Iwo Jima, Feb. 1945. Photo © TGST J. Sarno.

 PAGE 12–13: A panoramic photograph, most likely of a New York State Police unit in the Utica area, circa 1919.

 PAGE 14: A German postcard (circa 1915–1919) depicts a tracking war dog. Germany had an organized training system by 1870.

 PAGE 14–15: Karen Ogden and golden retriever Orion hot on a trail at a Jack Shuler man-trailing seminar. Photo © Jen Bidner.

 PAGE 16: USAF SSgt. Timothy Bellus and Manzo training on a tunnel obstacle. Photo © USAF Airman 1st Class Bradley A. Lail.

 PAGE 17: Sergeant and Ken Pullen follow an urban trail at a Jonni Joyce seminar in Zebulon, NC. Photo © Jen Bidner.

 PAGE 18: Vicki Pulver brings bloodhound Dixie to a scent article (a glove) at the start of a training trail. Photo © Jen Bidner.

 **PAGE 18:** Col. Richardson with tracking bloodhounds, from his book *War, Police & Watch Dogs*. (Wm. Blackwood & Sons, 1910).

 PAGE 19: Deja Vu, a German shepherd handled by Pat Thompson, following a trail at a Jack Shuler man-trailing seminar. Photo © Jen Bidner.

 PAGE 19: A portrait of the Riddler, a Malinois handled by Behesha Grist. He is both a trailing and narcotics dog. Photo © Jen Bidner.

 PAGE 20: Bloodhound Mika demonstrates her alert on handler Geri Messina of ILL-WIS SAR Dogs. Photo © Jen Bidner.

 PAGE 20–21: Year-old brown lab Buster and Bryan Ryndak of the ILL-WIS SAR Dog unit during a trailing training. Photo © Jen Bidner.

 PAGE 22: An American railroad detective training bloodhounds. Richardson's *War, Police & Watch Dogs* (Wm. Blackwood & Sons, 1910).

 PAGE 22: Jack Shuler's bloodhound Bentley, running after his quarry during training in Salem, Illinois. Photo © Jen Bidner.

PAGE 23: Jack Shuler, (a Deputy with Marion County Sheriffs Office) bonding with his bloodhound Bentley. Photo © Jen Bidner.

 PAGE 24: Bloodhound Dixie and her handler Vicki Pulver of ILL-WIS SAR Dogs pose for a portrait. Photo © Jen Bidner.

 PAGE 25: The Riddler, a Malinois handled by Behesha Grist, photographed while following a trail. Photo © Jen Bidner.

 PAGE 26: A German postcard circa 1919 showing an ambulance dog finding a wounded soldier. The handlers are in the distance.

 PAGE 27: Rukker, a cadaver dog handled by Lisa Mayhew (Investigator, Office of Chief Medical Examiner, NC). Photo © Jen Bidner.

 PAGE 28: A German postcard (circa 1915–1919) showing an Doberman pinscher ambulance dog preparing to look for wounded soldiers.

 PAGE 28: Panda, a border collie, shows off his agility training for handler Marci Larson at a Jonni Joyce Seminar. Photo © Jen Bidner.

   PAGE 29: European postcards (circa 1915–1919) showing dogs after they have found the wounded soldier.

 PAGE 30–31: Border collie Panda, handled by Marci Larson, quickly searches the wilderness for a victim during training. Photo © Jen Bidner.

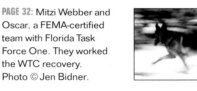 **PAGE 32:** Mitzi Webber and Oscar, a FEMA-certified team with Florida Task Force One. They worked the WTC recovery. Photo © Jen Bidner.

 PAGE 33: The author's German shepherd dog, Yukon, hones in on the victim as she follows a scent cone. Photo © Jen Bidner.

 PAGE 34: Gunner, a Fidelco German shepherd owned by Meleda and John Lowry. Photo © Jen Bidner.

 PAGE 34: An Air Force dog and handler patrol the Joint Readiness Training Center, Arkansas. Photo © MSGT Val Gempis.

 PAGE 35: The author and her dog Yukon have some fun "searching" for lost people at an amusement park. Photo © Jen Bidner.

PAGES 36–55: Photographs taken of the rescue and recovery efforts at the rubble of the World Trade Center towers after the terrorist attacks on September 11, 2001. Taken by FEMA photographer Andrea Booher.

PAGE 38: A French search and rescue dog team assists U.S. rescue efforts at the World Trade Center. Photo © Andrea Booher/FEMA.

 PAGE 39: Golden retriever Riley, handled by Chris Selfridge (PA TF-1) is trolleyed across the rubble. Photo © Preston Keres/US Navy.

 PAGE 40: CA TF-3 handler Shirley Hammond and Doberman Sunny climb onto the WTC rubble. Photo © Bri Rodriguez/FEMA.

 PAGE 42: Kinsay, a dog with TX TF-1, is treated by Dr. H Marie Suthers-McCable, DVM. Photo © Michael Rieger/FEMA.

 PAGE 42: Mike Scott (CA TF-8) and his black lab Billy traverse the dangerous rubble at the WTC site. Photo © Andrea Booher/FEMA.

 PAGE 43: Gus, a search dog from TN TF-1, goes through decontamination after working at the Pentagon. Photo © Jocelyn Augustino/FEMA.

 PAGE 47: A tired golden retriever search dog rests while recovery efforts take place a few feet away. Photo © Preston Keres/US Navy.

 PAGE 48: Kent Olson of Lakewood Washington and golden retriever Olson take a break at the WTC. Photo © Andrea Booher/FEMA.

PAGE 48: President George W. Bush greets search dogs and handlers at the World Trade Center site. Photo © Andrea Booher/FEMA.

 PAGE 49: A member of NM TF-1 works the Pentagon rubble site with her border collie. Photo © Jocelyn Augustino/FEMA.

 PAGE 49: Ed Apple and yellow lab Gus of TN TF-1 work in the rubble of the Pentagon. Photo ©Jocelyn Augustino/FEMA.

PAGE 51: Ann Wichmann and Jenner head out to start work on the rubble at the World Trade Center. Photo © Michael Rieger/FEMA.

 PAGES 50–53: Merlyn, Breeze, Jenner, Torie & Lance, five black Labrador retrievers handled by Ann Wichmann (CO-TF-1). Photo © Jen Bidner.

PAGE 54: A photograph of FEMA Missouri TF-1 handler at Oklahoma tornado disaster site in 1999. Photo © Andrea Booher/FEMA.

 PAGE 54-55: A photograph of FEMA New Mexico TF-1 handler at Oklahoma tornado disaster site in 1999. Photo © Andrea Booher/FEMA.

PAGE 56: Capt. Kerry W. Foster of Shreveport SAR and Ranger work New Orleans after Hurricane Katrina. Photo © Marvin Nauman/FEMA.

 PAGE 56: K9 Ranger of Shreveport SAR checks rubble after Hurricane Katrina. Photo © Marvin Nauman/FEMA.

 PAGE 57: A FEMA trained search dog is transported by helicopter into Hurricane Katrina recovery areas. Photo © Jocelyn Augustino/FEMA.

PAGE 58: Ski patrolman Keith Sternfels and his lab Chaco helped FEMA prepare for the 2002 Winter Olympics. Photo © Andrea Booher/FEMA.

 PAGE 58: Kim Gilmore's Belgian tervuren named Merak alerts on a victim in training. Flathead Co. SAR. Photo © Janet Yatchak.

PAGE 59: A photograph of ski patroller Jerry Balint's black Labrador retriever Coup. Coup found an avalanche victim in time to save him.

PAGE 60: Keno, a yellow Labrador retriever handled by Robin Siggers saved an avalanche victim. Photo © Fernie Ski Resort.

PAGE 61: The author's German shorthaired pointer Ajax (shown as a puppy) checks out his handler hidden in a snow cave. Photo © Jen Bidner.

PAGE 61: Merak and Mickey, Belgium tervurens handled by Kim Gilmore, Flathead Co. Search and Rescue. Photo © Janet Yatchak.

PAGE 61: An etching from a watercolor by Basil Bradley, entitled "On a Mission of Mercy." Reproduced in *The Graphic*, 1879.

PAGE 62: Sundance and handler Nan Lux (Search Dogs Northeast) at a Jonni Joyce Water Recovery Seminar. Photo © Jen Bidner.

PAGE 62: The author's German shorthair pointer Gottschalks Ajax alerts on training materials under the water. Photo © Anne Bidner.

PAGE 63: The author's German shepherd, Yukon, returning from a water search training. Photo © Meleda Wegner Lowry.

PAGE 64: Gordon setter Speedy, handled by Cil Chenevert, Leominster Emergency Management Agency. Photo © Jen Bidner.

PAGE 64: German shepherd Kizzy, handled by Cil Chenevert, Leominster Emergency Management Agency. Photo © Jen Bidner.

PAGE 65: The author's German shorthair pointer Gottschalks Ajax at age nine months, shown diving from a dock. Photo © Jen Bidner.

PAGE 65: The author's dogs, Ajax and Yukon, being rewarded with a game of swimming catch after training. Photo © Jen Bidner.

PAGE 66-67: Newfoundland dog named Junky pulls handler Celine Tonin and a "victim" to shore. Photo © Yves Forestier/CORBIS.

PAGE 67: A 19th century painting by Sir Edwin Henry Lanseer of a water dog after he rescued a young girl from the sea.

PAGE 68: Arkansas Game and Fish Commission K9 Jake, handled by Lt. Chris Carpenter. Photo © Keith Stephens/AR G&FC

PAGE 69: Arkansas Game and Fish Commission K9 Jake, handled by Lt. Chris Carpenter. Photo © Keith Stephens/AR G&FC.

PAGE 70: An illustration from an 1899 book entitled *Hector* that tells the story of the rescue dogs of the St. Bernard Pass in pictures and verse.

PAGE 70–71: Jeannie handled by Charm Gentry (WV K9 FACT) locates cadaver materials at a Jonni Joyce seminar. Photo © Jen Bidner.

PAGE 72: Oscar and handler Mitzi Webber (FL TF-1) walk up and "meet" a mannequin prior to training. Photo © Jen Bidner.

PAGE 72: Geist, handled by Tricia Heldmann (TASK-9), locates a scented mannequin during cadaver dog training. Photo © Jen Bidner.

PAGE 73: Alley, handled by Heather Roche, training at human remains detection at a Jonni Joyce seminar. Photo © Jen Bidner.

PAGE 73: Jonni Joyce training puppy Peaches (owned by Mary MacQueen, Nitro Golden Kennels). Photo © Jen Bidner.

 PAGE 74: Andrew Rebmann poses with German shepherd Griz. Rebmann is one of the authors of *The Cadaver Dog Handbook*.

 PAGE 74: Marcia Koenig and Coyote look for remains at the crash of KAL Flight 801 in Guam, as part of the Puget Sound Task Force, 1997.

 PAGE 75: Jeannie, handled by Charm Gentry (WV K9 FACT), looks up to locate cadaver scent in a tree. Photo © Jen Bidner.

 PAGE 75: Rukker and Lisa Mayhew (investigator with the office of the chief medical examiner, NC) train for cadaver. Photo © Jen Bidner.

PAGE 76: Whisky alerts on drugs hidden on this truck for Sgt. Mark Combes, Perry Oklahoma PD. Photo © Jen Bidner.

 PAGE 77: Whisky and Sgt. Mark Combes (Perry Police, OK) prepare for a day of patrol and narcotics detection. Photo © Jen Bidner.

 PAGE 78: Whisky vom Biebrstein, owned by Dr. Gayla Combes & Sgt. Mark Combes, Perry Oklahoma. Photo © Jen Bidner.

PAGE 78: Whisky vom Biebrstein rests near Sgt. Mark Combes's squad car, Perry (OK) Police Department. Photo © Jen Bidner.

 PAGE 79: Whisky alerts on drugs hidden on this truck for Sgt. Mark Combes, Perry Oklahoma PD. Photo © Jen Bidner.

PAGE 80-81: Ret. Officer Wm. Proulx, E. Hartford PD (CT) and Bruno. Photo © Alan Chaniewski, Special to the *Hartford Courant*.

PAGE 82: Ret. Officer Wm. Proulx, E. Hartford PD (CT). Photo © James A. Cortina, Director, Connecticut Police Working Dog Association (CPWDA).

 PAGE 83: Agility competition at the CT Police K9 Olympics. Photo © James A. Cortina, Director, CT Police Working Dog Association (CPWDA).

 **PAGE 83:** A Berkshire (England) police dog showing off its agility training, circa 1909. The London News Agency.

 PAGE 84–85: Three photos of Mighty Mony and handler Det. Jonni Joyce of the Raleigh-Durham International Airport Police. Photo © Jen Bidner.

PAGE 86: U.S. Marine Corp Bougainville, Solomon Islands from *Dogs at War* by Clayton G. Going (Macmillan Co., 1944).

 PAGE 86–87: Master at Arms 2nd Class Christopher C. Ray covers a "suspect" while Rocky disarms him. Photo © PH2 Michael J. Garrett.

 PAGE 88: SSG Richard Price and explosives dog in Bosnia-Herzegovina. Photo © SPC Tracy L. Hall-Leahy, United States Army.

PAGE 88: Cassie, an explosives detection dog, photographed at Lackland Air Force Base. Photo © MSGT Val Gempis.

  **PAGE 89:** A German draft dog pulls a a supply cart. The U.S. used draft dogs primarily to pull sleds in Greenland and Alaska.

PAGE 89: MA2 Christopher C. Ray, kennel supervisor, Rota Spain Security Dept., and Bobo. Photo by PH2 Michael J. Garrett/US Navy.

 PAGE 89: Master at Arms Second Class Stephen Johnson and his dog Barry apprehend a felon. Photo © PH2 M. Clayton Farrington.

 PAGE 90: An Air Force handler and dog check a West German Tornado aircraft at US Air Force ceremony. Photo © SSGT David Nolan.

 PAGE 90–91: A US Air Force dog and handler guard Lackland Air Force Base, Texas. Photo © Tech. Sgt. W. Boyd Belcher.

 PAGE 92: Andy and PFC Lansley, 1943, Bougainville, Solomon Islands, from *Dogs at War* by Clayton G. Going (Macmillan Co., 1944).

 PAGE 92: A WWI-era postcard (probably French) depicting an ambulance dog at a gravesite, mourning the loss of his handler.

 PAGE 92: US Air Force SSGT Derek Donahey plays with Rico at the Ramstein base, Germany. Photo © SSGT Ken Bergmann.

 PAGE 93: A US Air Force Malinois dog resting after training at Guantanamo Bay, Cuba. Photo © AMN Elizabeth Steward/US Air Force.

 PAGE 93: SSGT James Ming checks for narcotics and explosives at the Ramstein Air Force Base, Germany. Photo © SSGT Ken Bergmann.

 PAGE 92: Air Force security patrolman Troy Brashear inspects luggage with his narcotics dog. Photo © SST Glenn Justiss.

   PAGES 94–99: Eight images from the Customs/ATF Training Center, Front Royal, Virginia. Photos © James Tourtellote/ U.S. Customs.

 PAGE 100: The USDA's "Beagle Brigade" checks incoming passengers and cargo at U.S. land, sea, air, and cargo borders. Photos courtesy of the USDA.

 PAGE 101: Texanna of the USDA, handled by Wendy Beltz, shortly before her retirement in March, 2002. Photo © Jen Bidner.

 PAGES 102–103: USDA Wildlife Service handlers use Jack Russell terriers to search for brown tree snakes on Guam. Photos © Dan Vice/USDA.

 PAGE 104: Arkansas Game and Fish Commission K9 Doc, handled by Lt. Chris Carpenter. Photo © Keith Stephens/Arkansas G&FC.

PAGE 105: Arkansas Game and Fish Commission K9 Doc, handled by Cpl. Frankie Tucker. Photo © Kayti R. Isacksen/Arkansas G&FC.

PAGE 106–107: Comanche, handled by National Parks Service Ranger Janet Wilts, Grand Tetons. Photo © Jen Bidner.

 PAGE 108: Comanche, handled by National Parks Service Ranger Janet Wilts, Grand Teton National Park. Photo © Jen Bidner.

 PAGE 109: Three photos of Lt. Chris Carpenter and Cpl. Frankie Tucker, Arkansas Game and Fish Commission K9 Doc. Photo © Keith Stephens/ Arkansas G&FC.

 PAGE 111: Kathy Albrecht and weimaraner Rachel search for a missing box turtle. Photo courtesy of Kat Albrecht.

PAGE 112–113: Five labs owned by Ann Wichmann (CO TF-1). Three are FEMA-certified disaster dogs. Photo © Jen Bidner.

 PAGE 114: Willow and puppy Peaches, handled by Mary MacQueen (Nitro Golden Retrievers, Frewsburg, NY). Photo © Jen Bidner.

 PAGE 114: Group obedience at seminar hosted by Flathead Co. SAR and Western Montana Search Dogs. Photo © Charlie Tucker.

 PAGE 115: Weimaraner Parker gives Ryan a friendly kiss. Photo © Jen Bidner.

 PAGE 116: Golden retriever Gridley, owned by John & Meleda Lowry. Photo © Jen Bidner.

 PAGE 117: US Air Force SSGT James Ming with canine partner Ron at Ramstein Air Base in Germany. Photo © SSGT Ken Bergmann.

 PAGE 117: Fidelco's Taiz running at full speed. Handled by Tricia Heldmann, TASK-9 (Connecticut). Photo © Jen Bidner.

 PAGE 118: A portrait of Mika, a bloodhound handled by Geri Messina, ILL-WIS SAR Dogs unit. Photo © Jen Bidner.

 PAGE 119: Sonar, an 11-week-old lab, handled by Amir Findling (WNYSAR) gets used to wearing a search vest. Photo © Jen Bidner.

 **PAGE 120:** Fine is a black-and-white Deutsch Kurzhaar/ German shorthair pointer, owned by Dr. Gayla Combes. Photo © Jen Bidner.

 PAGE 120: The Riddler and Behesha Grist (Jack Shuler man-trailing seminars) play ball after training. Photo © Jen Bidner.

 PAGE 121: Black Labrador retriever, Jake, handled by Joseph Falman of TASK-9 (Connecticut). Photo © Jen Bidner.

 PAGE 121: Australian cattle dog, Rodeo, handled by Nancy Hook, REDS Team (Zebulon, NC). Photo © Jen Bidner.

 PAGE 121: USDA Animal and Plant Health Inspection Service canine, Texanna. Handled by Wendy Beltz. Photo © Jen Bidner.

 **PAGE 122–123:** Series of photos showing Bob Watson with Darshan, as Nancy Hook runs away (both are with REDS). Photo © Jen Bidner.

PAGE 127: Rottweiler Bevan poses in his search vest. Handled by Lucy Newton (Vermont). Photo © Jen Bidner.

About the Author

Jen Bidner

Jen Bidner is a volunteer K9 handler with Illinois-Wisconsin Search & Rescue Dogs (ILL-WIS), a not-for-profit canine unit that helps law enforcement agencies and fire departments in the Midwest find lost and missing people. She handles and trains her two search dogs, Ajax (shown) and Yukon. Bidner is the author of over a dozen books, including Is My Dog a Wolf? (Lark Books) and Love Your Dog Pictures: How to Photograph Your Pet with Any Camera (Amphoto). Photo © Meleda Wegner Lowry.

Visit www.illwissardogs.org for more information on SAR dogs.